John Guest is an ordained minister with more than 30 years' expe
ministry, and a professional clown. With over a quarter of a centu₁, ₂
working in local primary and secondary schools, he loves telling stories (particularly to
children) and spends much of his time in the ten schools around his parish. John
enjoys cooking, travel, languages and creative writing and occasionally admits to playing
the piano accordion. He is Rector of St Margaret's Parish Church, Stanford-le-Hope, in
Essex. He has also written *More Collective Worship Unwrapped* (Barnabas, 2010).

Dedicated with love to the thousands of children
it has been my privilege to work and play with but, above all,
to the two who call me Dad: Ben and Hannah

Acknowledgments

Let me start with some much-needed words of thanks. As I get older I discover more and more about the value of being grateful. I wish I'd known before what I know now, that developing a 'gratitude attitude' actually improves your emotional health. Ungrateful people are always miserable, even when they have everything. Grateful people are always happy, even when they have nothing.

I can never repay what I owe my family, Kim, Ben and Hannah, for all that they give to me in making me a better husband and father. I love you! Thank you.

Thanks to the church family here at St Margaret's and for my colleagues, Janice, Josh, Steve, Donald, Colin and David—particularly to Steve for his helpful insights and for introducing us to Jigsaw (I hope to see more of your work in print soon, Steve). To Pat Pickett, for help with typing, and to Sue Lester for painstakingly proofreading the manuscript. To my good friend, Dave Cooke, for setting out the score for 'God loves all of his children'. To 'Big Bob', better known as John 2. (How's your old muvver, right, John?) To Sue Doggett, my editor, and all my new friends at BRF. Thank you for your advice and encouragement.

To my wonderful schools here in Stanford-le-Hope: to the staff and pupils of Stanford Juniors and Infants, Arthur Bugler Juniors and Infants, Abbots Hall Juniors and Infants, Graham James and St Joseph's. To all the many schools it has been my privilege to work with over the years—you are great! Thank you.

Finally, to the many teachers whose patience and faith have shone like jewels along the path of my development. I never thanked you enough! To Simon and Rosemary Bourne and Chris Bulcraig, who helped lead me to Christ. To Margaret Redmond, head teacher and donkey wrangler extraordinaire. To my first Sunday school teacher, Ella Hutt, and to those two great saints who have now passed into the Presence—Muriel Coombes and Joyce Thornton. I owe you more than you know. And to the two whose discipling has been the longest—my parents, Joan and Ken.

And for you, Jesus, my teacher and my friend. All my collective worship is unwrapped and offered to you.

Text copyright © John Guest 2005
Illustrations copyright © Simon Smith 2005
The author asserts the moral right
to be identified as the author of this work

Published by
The Bible Reading Fellowship
15 The Chambers, Vineyard
Abingdon, OX14 3FE
United Kingdom
Tel: + 44 (0)1865 319700
Email: enquiries@brf.org.uk
Website: www.brf.org.uk
BRF is a Registered Charity
ISBN 978 1 84101 371 8
First published 2005
Reprinted 2008, 2009, 2011
10 9 8 7 6 5 4 3
All rights reserved

Acknowledgments
All scripture quotations are taken from the Contemporary English Version of the Bible published by HarperCollins Publishers, copyright © 1991, 1992, 1995 American Bible Society.

Performance and copyright
The right to perform *Collective Worship Unwrapped* drama material is included in the purchase price, so long as the performance is in an amateur context, for instance in church services, schools or holiday club venues. Where any charge is made to audiences, written permission must be obtained from the author, who can be contacted through the publishers. A fee or royalties may be payable for the right to perform the script in that context.

A catalogue record for this book is available from the British Library

Printed and bound in Singapore by Craft Print International Ltd

Collective Worship
Unwrapped

33 tried and tested story-based assemblies for primary schools

John Guest

Preface

Hello, everyone; welcome to our assembly! Welcome to *Collective Worship Unwrapped*.

Let me start by telling you a story. *Once upon a time...* a little girl stood at the gate of her primary school, welcoming the visitors one by one. 'Good morning, Mrs Jones,' she said. 'Hello, Mr Brown. Hi there, Miss Smith... Hello, God!' God, you might like to know, was me, visiting for one of my regular assemblies. It seems I made more than an impact on that little girl! I know that I don't look much like God and I'm not much taller than most primary school-age children, but I think there was an important point made in that little girl's conviction. When people like me go into local schools to meet classes and lead collective worship, we have the most incredible opportunity to make a difference. A head teacher I know once told me, 'Children are not vessels to be filled; they are lamps to be lit!' Those of us who work with children have the unique privilege of 'lighting lamps' when we form partnerships with our local schools.

The local trust I lead has the motto 'Building Bridges, Forging Friendships, Lighting Lamps', and this is essentially what we are doing when we meet with children, parents and teachers in our schools. The Balstonia Trust project (Stanford-le-Hope, Thurrock, South Essex) represents not just the convergence of need and opportunity in our schools but also the partnership we are developing between education, community and church. There is more on this and other contacts in the resource section at the end of this book.

There's a wealth of material currently available for all those of us involved in leading collective worship (or 'assemburly', as it is known to most younger children) in schools. However, as in so many areas, *what* you do is not always as important as *how* you do it. With over a quarter of a century behind me, working in local primary and secondary schools, I bring to the study a certain amount of expertise. Not that this makes me any kind of expert. As you probably know, an 'ex' is a has-been and a 'spurt' is a drip under pressure. Nevertheless, I've discovered certain principles that may be fairly universally applied when working with children and young people and that most blessed of creatures, the teacher.

This book sets out in a simple way the areas that need to focused on when considering school assemblies—the preparation, the environment wherein to 'perform' and how to use the material available. But, most of all, this book aims to show how to make assemblies *fun*!

By way of illustration, I've included a few of my own favourite assemblies. They are almost entirely original, although some of the inspiration for them has come from many sources and, above all, from the greatest storybook around—the Bible! Each section comes with a 'Bible link' to help ground the assembly in its biblical basis. There is reference to the suggested themes and an idea of what you will need to do the assembly. There is also a suggested prayer and a short selection of suitable songs. The key to where these songs may be found is on page 12. There are further suggestions of where to find help in the 'Resources' section at the end of the book. I very much hope that you will bring creativity and imagination to these assemblies and thus make them your own.

Enjoy the book and, above all, have fun!

John Guest

Contents

Appendix: Overhead visuals

Foreword

The act of collective worship fulfils many functions in the life of a primary school—it's a time for collective singing, an opportunity to celebrate individual or collective success and achievement, a 'noticeboard' for forthcoming events. Above all, it gives the whole school the chance simply to come together and meet as a unified group. The essence of the coming together is undoubtedly the sharing of a common experience, very often built around a core religious or moral theme. At the very heart of this is the need for the 'assembly taker' to be a good storyteller. Whether relating a story from first-hand knowledge or by retelling an existing text, the ability to hold an audience in the palm of one's hand is a rare gift.

I was therefore delighted when John asked me to write the Foreword for his book. I have had the pleasure over many years of listening and watching as he has enthralled our pupils with his storytelling. Whether it be in the guise of GOF the Clown, Indiana Johns or Mr Guest the Vicar, the children all keenly anticipate and thoroughly enjoy John's visits to school. Irrespective of whether they are four or eleven years old, they revel in the interactive nature of Honky the Donkey's retelling of 'The good Samaritan', and repeatedly chorus 'Yo! Henry!' in all the right places—and who of us can forget the sad but ultimately triumphant story of 'The little yellow line' as he finds his place in Christmas immortality.

Nobody can escape the participative nature of many of John's assemblies, and I have played many a walk-on role, including the carrying of the invisible bucket of invisible (but nonetheless very smelly) fertilizer to the far side of the hall in 'Invisible seeds'. This is interactive storytelling at its very best!

Unlike many other books of assembly stories, *Collective Worship Unwrapped* goes much further by including reference pages, Bible links, thematic index, relevant pictures for that all-important visual stimulus, and even a song to sing.

This book provides a wonderful resource for all headteachers' bookcases and staffroom resource shelves. I feel proud and privileged to be associated with it, and am sure that it will go a long way to enhance the storytelling skills of 'assembly takers' for many years of come.

Alan Clark,
Headteacher, Graham James Primary School,
Stanford-le-Hope

Introduction

This section includes ideas and suggestions for getting the most out of collective worship. However, the most important ingredient we can inject, apart from God's love, is ourselves! The important message of this book and others like it is that *we* are the bridge builders, the friendship forgers, the lamp lighters!

THE PRINCIPLES OF PREPARATION

Good preparation is vital. Any carpenter, painter or decorator will tell you that half the task is in the preparation. Get your wood or your wall or your window properly 'prepped' and you save yourself a lot of grief afterwards. You can usually tell the job that was inadequately done by the standard of the finish. Any activity that involves interaction with children needs to be carefully planned and prepared for.

Take conjuring, for instance. A good trick will need to be repeated over and over again before being tried out in the public arena. If it is to have maximum effect, the practitioner needs to cover every eventuality, so he or she will often practise dozens of times, even carrying out the procedure with their eyes closed. The better the preparation, the better the presentation. And the better the presentation, the better the penetration!

THE ESTABLISHMENT OF ENVIRONMENT

Nowadays, the society we live in is so busy and noisy that it is hard to find anywhere free from stress. Gordon McDonald, in his excellent book *Restoring your Spiritual Passion*, examines 'still times', 'safe places' and 'special friends' as three factors that can bring restoration. We would all recognize that school buildings need to be safe places. Open and public as they are, they need to be havens for the vulnerable. They also need to offer opportunities for quiet and reflection.

Most schools have a background of noise and busyness. Many of the children come from homes where stress is endemic. Noise and busyness are not all bad, but they are not everything. To be young *is* to be noisy and busy. There is so much to do, to learn and to experience, and today's culture pushes young people to learn faster, sooner. Information technology makes learning easier and more accessible, and changing moral standards allow younger children experiences that the children of yesterday would scarcely have dreamed of. For these and other reasons, it is vital to create an environment as well as a message for children. This environment will need to be an alternative environment to the one in which they are growing up. Collective worship is not the same as religious instruction, so the context of a school assembly is at least as important as the content. This concept is not always fully grasped, although, where it is, the effect is powerful and life-enhancing.

Today's propensity for polyphasing (doing more than one thing at the same time) has eclipsed our need for sacred space. Worship areas have become 'multi-purpose' and the secular has invaded the sacred to the point where the latter ceases to have meaning. A 'post-Christian' generation no longer realizes that 'spiritual' really means 'other' and to be 'holy' is to be 'set apart'. This is sad because the very thing our debt-ridden, stress-infected, designer label-conscious society needs is 'somewhere else' to go, 'something else' to do and, of course, 'someone else' to do it with. Incredible as it may seem, 'assemburly' may be one of the places where this can be achieved.

Collective worship, especially (but not exclusively) at the beginning of the school day, can provide a safe place where children can not only learn about God but experience him too. It's what Ofsted like to refer to as 'awe and wonder'. When we achieve that, we've struck gold.

Establishing a calm and peaceful environment in the area where collective worship is carried out is very important. School halls can often be adapted to create a positive spiritual environment. The establishment of the environment will relate very much to the senses, and the children will often respond positively to what they perceive as they enter the hall or designated classroom. If clear guidelines are established for what is acceptable behaviour in collective worship and those guidelines are consistently and sensitively underlined, then the 'otherness' of this time and space can be effectively communicated. Since assembly is also an ideal opportunity for notices (just like church services!) and also a chance to administer the 'telling off' where necessary, the 'otherness' aspect may be a little compromised, but this need not be a major problem.

Here, then, are some suggestions for establishing environment.

What we hear

This must come first as it will be the first sense impacted, even before the children enter. Music has a very powerful effect and should be used most sensitively. It can affect mood and attitude, and can enhance or destroy the environment right from the start. Music that is calming and relaxing is especially helpful for Foundation, Reception and early years children. Since first impressions are so powerful, the establishment of an environment that is different from where the children have just been sitting and what they have just been doing is very important. This is also a good reason why holding collective worship in a place other than where the children usually work is advisable.

What we see

There is huge scope through this medium. Pictures, colours, materials and objects can all convey positive experiences. Lighting will also be an important factor and should be used creatively. Closing drapes and blinds can be effective in establishing a 'holy space', but there also needs to be an element of 'openness'. Candles and fresh flowers can be very helpful. Lighting a candle is a very evocative act that the children themselves can be involved in. It can signify a moment of silence, reflection or prayer. Balloons and bubbles can also illustrate reflection or celebration. The overhead projector can display all kinds of images to enhance environment as well as illustrate talks and, if available, a video projector can display both still and moving images to enhance collective worship.

What we smell and taste

Smell and taste are senses that we do not usually associate with collective worship... or are they? Collective worship may involve tasting bread and wine and, in some situations, the very distinctive smell of incense.

Be very aware that these senses are at work, and use them in a positive way if you can. The smell of school dinner wafting under the shutters at the end of the hall may produce a positive (or negative!) reaction in both the sense of smell and the taste buds, but will it help the assembly? Although taste and smell may not be as important as sound and sight in establishing the environment for collective worship, they should still be taken into account. A pleasant or evocative smell in the hall, or an assembly that may involve tasting things, is certainly worth consideration.

What we feel

This sense will be active throughout an act of worship and long after it is over. I am utterly convinced that worship should be an enjoyable experience and, as such, it will involve that ghastly phrase, the 'feel good factor'. Put simply, if the children enjoy the assembly, it will be a good, positive and pleasant experience for them; if they don't, it won't! There are lots of factors associated with this sense. Perhaps thought could be given to how the children come in to assembly, where and how they sit and who they sit with. One of my local schools encourages the children to sit anywhere they like on the floor area, rather than putting them in rows by class or year grouping.

THE SKILL OF STORYTELLING

The telling of a story may form the major part of an act of collective worship. Although it is probably true to say that storytellers are born rather than taught, it is also true that we can pick up a lot of the basic skills of storytelling and use them in collective worship. In this book you will find a number of examples of assembly stories that have been used frequently in local schools, and an indication of some of the storytelling methods that are applied.

Learning how to speak and to appreciate the value of words will help us greatly in communicating with children and young people. Here are some pointers.

Know your story

Stories can be told or they can be read. If you are attempting the former, you will certainly need to have committed the tale to memory. If you are sufficiently accomplished, however, you will remember the highlights and use your imagination to fill in the gaps. Reading a story from a book can also have great value, although, if it is a picture book, you will want to find a way for the children to appreciate the artwork. Whether you read or tell, you will still need to prepare carefully. In most cases, the better the preparation, the better the story.

Engage your listeners

A good story, well told, will always engage the interest of the listeners. Nevertheless, you may want to use a variety of techniques to enhance this engagement. You may use various types of audience participation, such as responding to various words or phrases in the narrative. You might wish to include various comic interludes, such as getting obvious things wrong and having the children interrupt with correct information. This technique is often used in pantomime: 'He's behind you!' … 'Oh, no he isn't!' … 'Oh, yes he is!' and so on. You'll find this used to good effect with the 'Yo, Henry!' response in the story of 'Honky the Donkey' (pp. 36–37).

Repeat yourself

Narrative repetition is a classic technique used in storytelling and often appears in many of the traditional fairy tales. Think of the wicked queen's oft-repeated question to the magic mirror in 'Snow White and the seven dwarves', or the threefold response of the troll in 'The three Billy Goats Gruff'. Sometimes the technique of repetition is used to build suspense in a narrative: the children become more excited as they think, 'We've heard this before, we know what's going to happen!' There's an example of this technique in the story of 'Arthur and the magic fish' (pp. 71–73).

Simplify the tale

At Clown Camp, they teach the KISS principle: Keep It Simple, Stupid! Stories don't need to be overly complicated. The best ones usually have a very simple story line and development. Think of Grimm and Anderson and their classic fairy tales. Think also of the simplicity of the parables of Jesus and a good number of the other Bible stories. Making stories complicated, with ever more tortuous plots and twists in the narrative, works well in the written and read format, but a story that is told needs to be simple. Keep it simple and you hold the children's attention. Make it complicated and they may soon begin to lose interest.

Spice it up a bit!

The much overused phrase, 'Variety is the spice of life', is actually very good when you think about it. Variety saves us from bland mediocrity, and a good story can be ruined because it is just too boring and 'samey'. Spice can make a meal interesting, even surprising. Stories can do that too if they are imaginative, creative and varied. Among the examples in this book, you'll find familiar stories told from an unusual angle. For example, 'Big, Bad Brian the Lion' is the story of Daniel and the lions' den from a lion's perspective, while 'The little yellow line' approaches the Christmas story from the point of view of a road marking!

Variety is not just important in the content of the story but also in the way we tell it. Vary the pace of the narrative and the volume and, like the piquant spice or surprising chilli you bite into in your meal, the story jolts the children's listening capacities and deepens their appreciation of the event. Try starting a story with 'Once (pause) upon (pause) a (pause) time (pause) there (pause) was (pause) a (pause) …'. Or how about 'Once … once upon … once upon a … once upon a time … once upon a time there … once upon a time there was … once upon a time there was a …' and so on. See how variety can be used even in the simple classic start to a story.

Stay focused

The most successful jokes work best when they have a good start and a humorous punch line. What you put in between is up to your own creativity and imagination. Similarly, your stories will need a good start and finish, and will progress between those two points in a disciplined way. A good start is needed to grab the children's attention and a good 'punch line' will, you hope, leave them thinking and wanting more. The journey between beginning and ending will naturally employ the techniques listed above but it must progress consistently. For example, in the story of 'Arthur and the magic fish', the weather must deteriorate consistently and the opulence of Isabelle's accommodation must increase consistently (albeit to a ridiculous level). This attention to details requires practice and care but ensures a high level of excellence in the telling of the tale. Focus in narrative should also ensure that we retain the interest and approval of the children.

Smile!

You'd be surprised how much difference a positive attitude can make. Short or long, biblical or secular, tell your tale with vibrancy, passion and enthusiasm, and even the sorriest story will animate your audience and raise their interest levels significantly. Believe in what you are doing and project your enjoyment of the story and you will hold your listeners in the palm of your hand.

When I was younger and had a tendency to embellish my experiences with rather fanciful narrative,

I was told sharply, 'Don't tell stories!' I think what was meant was 'Don't tell lies', and with that I heartily concur. Stories, on the other hand, are not lies, even though many of them are not true. If stories had to be 'true', we would require Jesus to prove that the good Samaritan, the farmer and the prodigal son all existed independently of the parables in which they appeared. No—the fictional nature of parables and stories makes them no less valuable to us. They continue to be a vital resource in the communication of education, entertainment and encouragement.

THE READINESS OF RESOURCES

When I first started taking 'assemburly', back in the 1970s, you really had to make it up as you went along, coming up with your own ideas and trusting in the innate power of the story. Nowadays, I'm glad to say, there is a veritable treasure-house of material available to use with various age groups. Some of this, I'm pleased to say, you can discover within the pages of this book.

Most of the collective worship material available in book form has been written to be used. Provided you check your copyright cover, permissions and so on, it is fine just to go ahead and use it. It is well worthwhile taking a stroll around your local Christian bookshop and leafing through some of the resources that are on offer. The internet is also a very useful source of collective worship material: many Christian publishing houses and children's organizations have excellent websites. The Church of England diocesan children's and schools' advisers will also have much to offer.

It is, of course, very important to be creative in the use of other people's material. Anybody can simply rehash someone else's ideas, repeating parrot-fashion what someone else has put together. The best value gained from using someone else's material is to let it be a springboard for your own thoughts and ideas. Let's face it, you're never going to be able to do what the original writer did quite as well as they did it, because the context will be completely different. The stories and ideas gleaned from a variety of books are always better adapted to the local scene and the children you are addressing. It is only common courtesy to credit the originator of the idea where that is appropriate, but there is no reason why those same ideas should not encourage our own creative abilities to rise. Use the assemblies I've set out in this book—that's what they're there for—but don't just copy them verbatim. Use your imagination, your own adapted visual aids, your own voice characterization and so on. Your collective worship will need to be as individual and unique as the school you work in.

The best resource of all, of course, is the Bible. When I first introduce people to the Bible, I remind them that it is not actually a book but a library. There are 66 books in this library, all of them with their own particular appeal. The Bible is far more than just a storybook, history book, poetry book or theology book: it is a huge resource that encompasses all these things and a very great deal more.

Each of the assemblies set out in this book begins with a 'Bible link' so that you have a passage from the Bible to look at in preparation for the assembly. The reference is given for each passage, accompanied by an abridged text. Sometimes it is good to read the Bible aloud to children or to listen to someone else read it, live or recorded. It is also good to get the children to read aloud with you a portion of the Bible. Modern translations of the Bible are invaluable and it may also be helpful to look at modern paraphrases. The translation I use throughout this book is the Contemporary English Version (CEV). One huge resource on the internet is the website www.bible.com, which is operated by the large US publishing house Zondervan. I have found many fascinating pages on this site and a host of Bible translations in many languages.

Never underestimate the huge resource we have in the Bible! I never tire of reading it, especially now that I've managed to download the whole thing on to my PDA (that's a tiny little notepad-sized computer, for all you technophobes!). I even enjoy reading the passages I know well and the stories that are so familiar. Somehow, there's a new meaning, nuance or message to be gleaned every time. In this book, you'll find three separate assemblies based on the well-known 'Road to Emmaus' story from Luke 24, each with a slightly different emphasis.

The Bible itself tells us to 'do your best to win God's approval as a worker who doesn't need to be ashamed and who teaches only the true message' (2 Timothy 2:15). We owe it to ourselves and to the children we work with to become good students of the Bible, like avid miners, digging deep into it to unearth all the treasures it holds. But a word of warning: once you set yourself to examine and study the word of God, you will never be the same—for the Bible is the only volume I know that reads its reader.

Key to songs

The songs listed in each section are taken from the following books:

Junior Praise (JP), Peter Horrobin and Greg Leavers (Marshall Pickering, ISBN 978 0 551 01293 6)

KidsSource: Super Songs for Church and School (KS), Captain Alan Price CA (Kevin Mayhew, ISBN 978 1 84003 310 6)

Songs of Fellowship for Kids (SFK) (Kingsway Music, ISBN 978 0 85476 735 9)

Sounds of Living Waters/Fresh Sounds (SOLW), Betty Pulkingham and Jeanne Harper (Hodder and Stoughton, ISBN 978 0 340 23262 0)

Tinderbox—6 Songs for Children (TB), Sylvia Barratt and Sheena Hodge (A&C Black, ISBN 978 0 7136 2170 9)

The song below, 'God loves all of his children', is very useful for quietening a noisy group. Ideally, it should be sung unaccompanied (once you've mastered the tune) with the children clicking their fingers in time to the beat. The song should begin quietly, get louder and louder and then softer and softer, with the children ending (we hope) in complete silence. It is also a good song for using when there are no musical resources.

God loves all of his children

God loves all of his children

God loves all of his children

He gives them all of his love

He gives them all of his love.

God loves all of his children

Words and music anon. Copyright control

Key Stage One
assemblies

The Toolshed Gang

The following six assemblies are designed primarily for Key Stage One. Each assembly is strongly story-based and character-orientated and uses everyday items that can be picked up in the home, garage or garden shed as visual aids.

Even in this technological age, many children still find tools fascinating and enjoy working with their hands. In these stories, the characters can be produced and children can hold them—under careful supervision, of course. In addition, and to aid visual impact, the Appendix on page 115 provides pictures of the main characters, which may be photocopied or scanned into a computer for projection. The concept of the 'Master Builder' owes nothing, in this instance, to Henrik Ibsen but everything to the New Testament.

Safety hints: Be very careful when allowing the children to handle the tools, especially the chisel and the pliers. The chisel should be masked in a case and children should be discouraged from opening and shutting the pliers. Take the opportunity to stress the importance of tools and the dangers of using them improperly. This could be a good opportunity to involve the school caretaker or maintenance operative, or even an appropriate and available parent who works with tools.

The Toolshed Gang:

The four friends

 ## Bible link

1 Corinthians 12:12–31

The body of Christ has many different parts, just as any other body does… Suppose a foot says, 'I'm not a hand, and so I'm not part of the body.' Wouldn't the foot still belong to the body? Or suppose an ear says, 'I'm not an eye, and so I'm not part of the body.' Wouldn't the ear still belong to the body? If our bodies were only an eye, we couldn't hear a thing. And if they were only an ear, we couldn't smell a thing. But God has put all parts of our body together in the way that he decided is best… It takes many parts to make a single body. That's why the eyes cannot say they don't need the hands. That's also why the head cannot say it doesn't need the feet… God put our bodies together in such a way that even the parts that seem the least important are valuable. He did this to make all parts of the body work together smoothly, with each part caring about the others. If one part of our body hurts, we hurt all over. If one part of our body is honoured, the whole body will be happy.

 ## Visual aids

❖ A toolbox with a selection of tools including a large hammer, a chisel, a screwdriver and a pair of pliers.
❖ Alternatively, or preferably in addition, pictures of the characters to show or project (see page 115).

 ## Main themes

Friendship and co-operation

Further topics covered

Unity, mutual respect, the Church, identity.

 ## Prayer

Dear God, thank you for making each of us just the way we are. We are each special. There's only one of each of us and you love us just like this. Thank you, God. Amen

 ## Songs

I'm special (KS)
Jesus put this song (KS)
Thank you for my friends (TB)

FOLLOW-UP

Find out children's likes and dislikes in terms of school subjects, hobbies, sports and games. This could be done as a circle time with each child contributing one like and one dislike. In almost every case, a child will be good at doing the thing they like. Gently widen the discussion to take in why some people are good at some things and some at others. You could highlight a famous sports personality and consider why they might not be a particularly good singer or guitarist. You could focus on a pop group and consider how good they might be at sport or games. The discussion could be widened in this area, depending on how much time is available. If you have the expertise and equipment, you could explain how different instruments work well playing together in harmony, but not everyone can play every instrument.

Talk about how God makes us all different, with different likes and dislikes. When we compare ourselves to others, we should not become vain or jealous. We should work together as a team: Together Everyone Achieves More.

Once upon a time, not so long ago, in a shed at the bottom of the garden, was a toolbox. I don't know its name but it was big and it was strong and it had many tools inside it. It belonged to the Master Builder, and he loved it and all the tools inside it.

Four of the tools were particularly important. They were good friends who did a lot of work together. Let's meet them, shall we?

(As you introduce the four main characters, you can take them out of the toolbox and/or show them on the screen.)

First, there was Billy the Big Hammer. He was strong and liked working but was inclined to be a bit hard-headed. He was a lot bigger than Sally the Small Hammer, who was only used for the smaller and more delicate jobs. Next there was Clara the Chisel. She was tall and slim but also had rather a sharp tongue. After her came Sammy the Screwdriver. He could

turn himself to most jobs and was particularly useful at getting in and out of scrapes. Finally, there was Paula the Pliers. Although she was rather short and fat, once she got a grip on something she never let go!

One fine day, the four friends were sitting quietly on the workbench after a particularly busy morning. They were all rather tired and quite a bit grumpy. 'I'm quite worn out,' complained Clara the Chisel with her sharp tongue. 'It's all right for you, Sammy, with your flat, blunt end. All you have to do is lie there in the Master's hand. I get pushed right in! Really deep! I'm exhausted.'

'Nothing to do?' replied Sammy crossly. 'You ought to try getting a screw out when it's stuck. Paula has no problem! With her sharp grip she just gives one big pull and out it comes! I wish I had her job.'

'You can have it!' said Paula. 'I'd much rather have Billy's. He's so big and strong. He gets all the best jobs to do. I hate being

Reproduced with permission from *Collective Worship Unwrapped* published by BRF 2005 (978 1 84101 371 8) www.barnabasinschools.org.uk

small and fat. I wish I was a hammer!'

Billy the Big Hammer sat up straight on the workbench. 'What's so good about being a hammer? What do you get to do all day? Hammer! Hammer, hammer, hammer! Banging in nails—that's all I do. Now, if I were a chisel, for instance…' said Billy. 'There's a *real* tool! You get to cut and scrape and rout and shape—such a lot of different jobs. A lot more interesting than hammering!'

(During this conversation, find a way to emphasize which of the tools is talking. You could get the child with the relevant tool to hold it up and/or show the particular tool on the screen.)

'Hang on a minute,' shouted Sammy, jumping to his foot. 'What if we all changed places? Billy could do all the chiselling and shaping, and Clara could become a screwdriver instead. Paula could become a big strong hammer, and I could become what I've always wanted to be—Sammy the Pliers!'

The four friends agreed that this was an excellent idea, so, when the Master Builder came back from his lunch, they all set about doing their new jobs. And do you know what? It was a disaster! Billy was completely the wrong shape for chiselling and, besides, he had no sharp edges to cut cleanly into the wood. On the other hand, Clara with her sharp foot was hopelessly unsuited to putting screws in and out. At one point, trying really hard to get a job done, she slipped and gashed the Master's hand! Paula realized as soon as the Master Builder started using her to bang in nails that she did *not* like being a Big Hammer. After a very short time, her head

started to ache, and her pincer mouth, so useful for pulling out stubborn fixings, really began to hurt quite badly. And as for Sammy, whose idea it was in the first place… he soon realized that to be a pair of pliers needed two legs and gripping mouth, and he had only one leg and no gripping mouth at all!

At the end of the day, the four friends lay exhausted on the workbench and realized how silly they had been. None of them had been able to do any of the other's jobs properly and the Master Builder had got hardly any of his work done. 'I should never have tried to be a chisel,' said Billy. 'I'm made to be a hammer, and a hammer I should be.'

'And I should stick to being a chisel,' said Clara. 'There's no one can chisel like Clara the Chisel.'

Sammy and Paula agreed. 'I think tomorrow we should go back to doing what we were made for,' said Paula.

And do you know what? That's exactly what they did!

Reproduced with permission from *Collective Worship Unwrapped* published by BRF 2005 (978 1 84101 371 8) www.barnabasinschools.org.uk

The Toolshed Gang:

Oily Fred

 Bible link

Ephesians 4:1–16

Always be humble and gentle. Patiently put up with each other and love each other. Try your best to let God's Spirit keep your hearts united. Do this by living at peace. All of you are part of the same body… Christ has generously divided out his gifts to us… Christ chose some of us to be apostles, prophets, missionaries, pastors, and teachers, so that his people would learn to serve and his body would grow strong… Christ holds [the body] together and makes all its parts work perfectly, as it grows and becomes strong because of love.

Visual aids

❖ A toolbox with a selection of tools including a large hammer, a chisel, a screwdriver, a pair of pliers and a large can of oil (ideally as dirty and as oily as possible).

❖ Alternatively, or preferably in addition, pictures of the characters to show or project.

Helpful hint

Take care with the dirty oil can. You could provide a small pair of old industrial or garden gloves for the child who carries the can.

 Main themes

The Holy Spirit and prejudice.

Further topics covered

Personal growth and development, racism.

 Prayer

Dear God, thank you for giving us your Holy Spirit to help us every day. Thank you that you help us to follow Jesus. Amen

 Songs

Give me oil in my lamp (KS)
The Spirit lives to set us free (KS)
This is the day (JP)

FOLLOW-UP

Use a small flask of oil as a visual aid. Baby oil or olive oil are probably best.

Ask the children to give you a list of different types of oil. You could write them up on a whiteboard. Ask for suggestions as to what oil might be used for.

Get a few volunteers to come and pour out some oil on to a saucer and then dip their fingers in it. What does it look like… smell like… feel like? *(Have some tissues and/or kitchen roll handy for sticky fingers!)*

How did Oily Fred help the tools? Can you think of other ways that oil can help machinery?

In the Bible it tells us that God gives his Holy Spirit to help Christians in their daily lives. One of the symbols for the Holy Spirit is oil. Can you think of any ways that the Holy Spirit might be just like Oily Fred?

Once upon a time, not so long ago, in a shed at the bottom of the garden, was a toolbox. I don't know its name but it was big and it was strong and it had many tools inside it. It belonged to the Master Builder, and he loved it and all the tools inside it.

Four of the tools were particularly important. They were good friends who did a lot of work together. Let's meet them, shall we?

(As you introduce the four main characters, you can take them out of the toolbox and/or show them on the screen.)

First, there was Billy the Big Hammer. He was strong and liked working but was inclined to be a bit hard-headed. He was a lot bigger than Sally the Small Hammer, who was only used for the smaller and more delicate jobs. Next there was Clara the Chisel. She was tall and slim but also had rather a sharp tongue. After her came Sammy the Screwdriver. He could turn himself to most jobs and was particularly useful at getting in and out of scrapes. Finally, there was Paula the Pliers. Although she was rather short and fat, once she got a grip on something she never let go!

One fine day, the four friends were on the workbench in the tool shed once again, talking about their day. 'Well, I've had a terrible day!' complained Paula the Pliers. 'I've been really stiff and it has been so hard to open and shut my mouth. I think I've got arthritis.'

'Tools don't get arthritis,' said Sammy the Screwdriver. 'Besides, I'm surprised you had trouble opening your mouth!'

'Don't be so unkind,' replied Paula. 'The worst part of the day was bumping into Oily Fred. Look at me—I'm filthy!'

'Not Oily Fred,' snorted Clara the Chisel. 'He's always rubbing up against me. I hate him! He's *so* dirty!'

'Don't talk to me about that dirty, smelly, disgusting Oily Fred,' shouted Sammy. 'There I was today, minding my own business, trying to get out a particularly stiff wood screw, when up pops Oily Fred and starts dribbling all over my work! What a mess!'

'Oily Fred is horrible,' complained Paula. 'Just look at the mess he's made of my lovely shiny mouth. What do you think, Billy?'

Billy the Big Hammer looked up from the workbench. 'I think you've got it all wrong,' he said.

Clara, Sammy and Paula all looked at Billy in amazement. 'Wrong?!' they said. 'How can we be wrong?' said Clara. 'Just look at the stains Oily Fred has made on my blade. He's just so… so… so oily!'

'When you've been around as long as I have,' said Billy, 'you'll understand just how

Reproduced with permission from *Collective Worship Unwrapped* published by BRF 2005 (978 1 84101 371 8) www.barnabasinschools.org.uk

important Oily Fred is in the tool shed. Why, the Master uses him everywhere. If it wasn't for Oily Fred, none of us would be able to do our jobs properly.'

'But he's so dirty,' complained Paula, 'and he's always dribbling on us.'

'He's not dirty,' replied Billy. 'He's just oily, that's all. And his oil is really important to help us tools work. Tell me, Paula, did you work any better after you'd bumped into Oily Fred?'

'Come to think of it,' said Paula, 'now you mention it, and just by the way—yes! My mouth opened and shut much more easily and I wasn't nearly as stiff!'

'Did that wood screw come out more easily, Sammy?' asked Billy.

'Well,' said Sammy slowly, 'as a matter of fact, it did! But what's that got to do with Oily Fred?'

'Yes,' interrupted Clara with her sharp tongue, 'and what about getting me all dirty?'

'Not dirty,' replied Billy the Big Hammer,

'just… oily! You see—that's the whole point. Oily Fred's oil is what helps us to do our jobs properly. He loosens Paula when she gets stiff, and frees Sammy's screws when they're difficult to get out. And he keeps tools like Clara and me clean and useful and stops us going rusty. So don't think badly of Oily Fred—he's really important. Heads up, tools! Here he comes now.'

Just at that moment, Oily Fred appeared on the bench beside them. His battered old can was grubby and sticky and displayed a large sign saying '3-in-one', but somehow he seemed now to the four friends to have a special charm all of his own.

''Ello, Billy,' said Oily Fred in his funny squeaky voice. ''Ello, Clara, 'ello, Sammy, 'ello, Paula. You four mind if oi come and snuggle up close to you?'

'We don't mind at all,' said the four friends together. 'We like you! You come and snuggle up with us any time you like! What would we do without you? Thank you, Oily Fred!'

The Toolshed Gang:

Pontifex the Power Saw

 ## Bible link

John 15:1–17

Jesus said to his disciples: I am the true vine, and my Father is the gardener… Just as a branch cannot produce fruit unless it stays joined to the vine, you cannot produce fruit unless you stay joined to me. I am the vine, and you are the branches. If you stay joined to me, and I stay joined to you, then you will produce lots of fruit. But you cannot do anything without me… Stay joined to me and let my teachings become part of you… I have loved you, just as my Father has loved me. So remain faithful to my love for you… Now I tell you to love each other, as I have loved you.

Visual aids

❖ A toolbox with a selection of tools including a large hammer, a chisel, a screwdriver, a pair of pliers, a large can of oil (ideally as dirty and as oily as possible), and a power saw.
❖ Alternatively, or preferably in addition, pictures of the characters to show or project.

Helpful hint

Make sure you have somewhere to plug in the power saw at the right moment.

> **Be safe:** Don't let any of the children handle the power saw!

 ## Main themes

Gifts and abilities.

Further topics covered

Guidance, help, doing your best, power.

 ## Prayer

Dear God, please keep us close to you and help us to do your will. Never let go of us, and show us how to serve you and do your special work. Thank you, God. Amen

 ## Songs

I want to be a tree that's bearing fruit (KS)
One more step along the world I go (KS)
This little light of mine (KS)

FOLLOW-UP

Have a selection of unusual tools for the children to look at and handle carefully. Pick tools that are old-fashioned and that have strange names. You could go beyond the workshop to domestic implements that are unusual. Ask the children to guess the names of the implements and what they might have been used for. You could have a competition (with an inexpensive prize) for anyone who guesses the names. Write the names on the board.

Talk about tools or appliances the children may have used. Share any amusing stories you have about implements that went wrong. Discuss the importance of using tools and appliances correctly. What is the best way to learn? (Read the instructions or ask an expert.)

Explain how Christians trust God by reading his instruction book (the Bible) and by talking to him (prayer) and by trying to stay close to him, just like Oily Fred suggests in the story!

Once upon a time, not so long ago, in a shed at the bottom of the garden, was a toolbox. I don't know its name but it was big and it was strong and it had many tools inside it. It belonged to the Master Builder, and he loved it and all the tools inside it.

Four of the tools were particularly important. They were good friends who did a lot of work together. Let's meet them, shall we?

(As you introduce the four main characters, you can take them out of the toolbox and/or show them on the screen.)

First, there was Billy the Big Hammer. He was strong and liked working but was inclined to be a bit hard-headed. He was a lot bigger than Sally the Small Hammer, who was only used for the smaller and more delicate jobs. Next there was Clara the Chisel. She was tall and slim but also had rather a sharp tongue. After her came Sammy the Screwdriver. He could turn himself to most jobs and was particularly useful at getting in and out of scrapes. Finally, there was Paula the Pliers. Although she was rather short and fat, once she got a grip on something she never let go!

One fine morning, the four friends were all inside the toolbox together, waiting to begin the day's work. As usual, they were showing off a bit. 'Just you wait till I get started,' boasted Billy the Big Hammer. 'I'm going to hammer and hammer and hammer. I'll be a better hammer than any hammer!'

'And I'll chisel better than any chisel,' said Clara the Chisel. 'I'm the best chisel in the tool shed!'

'I can't wait to get to work,' boasted Sammy the Screwdriver. 'I'm the best tool in the

whole toolbox. Watch out, screws—here I come!'

'And anything that needs pulling out, twisting off or tightening up,' yelled Paula the Pliers, 'has got me to reckon with. I can do just about anything!'

'Can you now?' said a deep voice from a dark corner of the box. 'I wonder if you can match the skill of… Pontifex the Power Saw?' And with that a strange tool emerged from the dark recesses of the toolbox. He was dark blue and silver and glistening with oil. He had a big head like Billy, and a long sharp nose like Clara and Sammy. And… yes… he even had some strong gripping teeth like Paula. To add to all this, he had a long black tail with a small box on the end.

'What a peculiar-looking tool,' whispered Sammy to Paula. 'He's like nothing I've ever seen before.'

Reproduced with permission from *Collective Worship Unwrapped* published by BRF 2005 (978 1 84101 371 8) www.barnabasinschools.org.uk

'We can do anything better than you can,' said Clara with her sharp tongue. 'Why, you don't even look like a proper tool!'

But the strange blue and silver object didn't say any more. He just lay quietly in the box until the Master Builder came to take all the tools to work.

When the four friends got to the task set for them, they found a long thick piece of wood that the Master Builder needed dividing. All four jumped in without hesitation, Billy hammering and banging for all he was worth, Paula holding the wood as tightly as possible in her metal jaws, Clara diving in and out of the wood with her long sharp tongue and Sammy jumping from side to side, offering advice to anyone who would listen. After ten minutes of frantic activity, none of the tools seemed to have made any impression on the wood; it lay as undivided as before.

In the meantime, the Master Builder took the tail of the strange blue and silver tool called Pontifex and plugged the box into three small holes in the wall. At once, Pontifex the Power Saw began to hum and buzz, and his long metal blade began to whiz up and down so fast! In no time at all, the swiftly moving blade cut neatly through the wood and the two halves fell apart, perfectly divided.

Later that evening, the four friends looked in on Oily Fred as he sat in his special place on the tool shed shelf. They asked him to explain the strange thing they had all seen that day, and what was so special about Pontifex the Power Saw. 'Well, my little friends,' wheezed Oily Fred in his strange squeaky voice, 'it's not so much Pontifex himself as the power he uses.'

'Whatever does that mean?' asked Billy the Big Hammer.

'His long black tail is what the Master uses to channel power into Pontifex,' replied Oily Fred. 'So long as he is plugged into the power socket, Pontifex the Power Saw can work better or faster than any tool in the toolbox!'

'That's not fair!' complained Clara. 'We don't have long black tails like that. How can we work better for the Master?'

'I'll let you into a special secret,' said Oily Fred. 'We can all have special power if we stay in the Master's hand. You don't *have* to be a power tool and have a long black tail, but you do need to stay close to the Master Builder and let him use you in his way. Whatever you do and whoever you are—stay in the Master's hand!'

Reproduced with permission from *Collective Worship Unwrapped* published by BRF 2005 (978 1 84101 371 8) **www.barnabasinschools.org.uk**

The Toolshed Gang:

Timmy the Tile Cutter

 ## Bible link

1 Corinthians 12:12–25

The body of Christ has many different parts, just as any other body does... It takes many parts to make a single body... God put our bodies together in such a way that even the parts that seem the least important are valuable. He did this to make all parts of the body work together smoothly, with each part caring about the others.

Visual aids

❖ A toolbox with a selection of tools including a large hammer, a chisel, a screwdriver, a pair of pliers and a tile cutter.

FOLLOW-UP

This assembly provides a good opportunity to do a circle time session on difference. Pass an object around the circle: children can speak while holding the object and, when they stop speaking, they pass it on. Remember the ground rules: no one is allowed to comment on someone else's words and no one is allowed to be negative or unkind about someone else. Everyone promises to say nothing outside the circle after it is finished.

Ask some questions about what makes us different and whether difference matters. Consider some of the advantages of being different. What would an orchestra be like if all the instruments were the same and all played exactly the same tune?

Be prepared to handle the issues of prejudice and bullying. Encourage the children to talk to God, and tell a teacher or a parent, if they know of bullying taking place.

❖ Alternatively, or preferably in addition, pictures of the characters to show or project.

Helpful hint
As the tile cutter is a rather specialist tool, you may need to do a bit of searching at your local hardware store. It is important to get a specialist tool, as the whole purpose of the story rests on the tool being 'out of the ordinary'.

> **Be safe:** Take the opportunity to stress the importance of tools and the dangers of using them improperly.

 ## Main themes

Respect and identity.

Further topics covered
Friendship and co-operation, being special, prejudice, bullying, difference.

 ## Prayer

Dear God, help us to realize that no matter who we are, what we look like or where we come from, we are special to you. Thank you, God. Amen

 ## Songs

If I were a butterfly (KS)
I'm special (KS)
You may think I'm so young (KS)

Once upon a time, not so long ago, in a shed at the bottom of the garden, was a toolbox. I don't know its name but it was big and it was strong and it had many tools inside it. It belonged to the Master Builder, and he loved it and all the tools inside it.

Four of the tools were particularly important. They were good friends who did a lot of work together. Let's meet them, shall we?

(As you introduce the four main characters, you can take them out of the toolbox and/or show them on the screen.)

First, there was Billy the Big Hammer. He was strong and liked working but was inclined to be a bit hard-headed. He was a lot bigger than Sally the Small Hammer, who was only used for the smaller and more delicate jobs. Next there was Clara the Chisel. She was tall and slim but also had rather a sharp tongue. After her came Sammy the Screwdriver. He could turn himself to most jobs and was particularly useful at getting in and out of scrapes. Finally, there was Paula the Pliers. Although she was rather short and fat, once she got a grip on something she never let go!

One fine morning, the four friends were on the workbench together, getting ready for the day's work. 'Have you seen the newest tool?' said Clara. 'He looks *really* odd!'

'I know,' replied Sammy the Screwdriver. 'He's got funny little red legs and the strangest face you ever did see. He's called Timmy the Tripe Cutter or something!'

'Watch out,' called Billy the Big Hammer. 'Here he comes now!'

Two little red legs appeared over the edge of the toolbox, and a strange-looking tool dropped down beside the four friends. 'Hello, Timmy the Tripe Cutter,' sniggered Paula the Pliers. 'And how are you today?'

All the tools laughed out loud at the strange little creature.

'Very well, thank you,' replied the new tool in a funny high-pitched voice, 'but I'm not a tripe cutter, if you please, sir. I'm Timmy the *Tile* Cutter!'

'A tile cutter? A tile cutter! Whatever next?' snapped Clara with her sharp tongue. 'You certainly are the strangest-looking tool I've ever seen! I don't see how you'd be any use to the Master Builder at all! You haven't got a big strong head for banging nails! You can't grip much with that silly little mouth, and your feet are the wrong shape for extracting screws. And you're certainly not sharp enough to cut wood—like I can!'

The little tile cutter didn't say anything. He just looked very, very sad.

Reproduced with permission from *Collective Worship Unwrapped* published by BRF 2005 (978 1 84101 371 8) www.barnabasinschools.org.uk

After a while, the Master Builder came and bundled all his tools into the toolbox and set off for his next job.

'I wonder what it will be,' said Billy. 'I hope it's building something where I can go hammer, hammer, hammer!'

'Ooo, yes,' said Paula, 'and where I can use my strong teeth to pull out any nails that go wonky!'

'And maybe I'll get to put some screws in, or even get them out,' said Sammy. 'I love it when we can all work together. We're a great team, us four!' And he quite deliberately turned his back on poor Timmy, who was crouching in a corner of the toolbox.

They arrived at the job and—surprise, surprise—it was a bathroom that needed fitting. Billy the Big Hammer nearly leaped out of the box to help, but the Master Builder set him aside. Clara the Chisel strained to be first, but the Master Builder put her down next to Billy. Sammy was sure he would be needed as he was on most jobs, but the Master Builder set him aside also.

At first, Paula thought she would get the job, as the Master Builder took her in his hand with a large blue tile, but then he laid her aside next to Billy, Clara and Sammy.

'Now, where's my little tile cutter?' said the Master Builder. 'Ah, there you are! Just what I need for cutting these tricky bathroom tiles.'

He lifted Timmy the Tile Cutter out of the toolbox and started cutting all the tiles he needed to finish the bathroom. Meanwhile, Billy the Big Hammer, Clara the Chisel, Sammy the Screwdriver and Paula the Pliers lay unused by the side of the toolbox. The Master would use them another day, I'm sure, but today was Timmy's day, and I think they all learned an important lesson.

Have you learned it too?

Reproduced with permission from *Collective Worship Unwrapped* published by BRF 2005 (978 1 84101 371 8) **www.barnabasinschools.org.uk**

The Toolshed Gang:

Reggie Rough and Ritchie Rasp

 **Bible link**

1 Peter 2:1–10

Stop being hateful! Stop trying to fool people, and start being sincere. Don't be jealous or say cruel things about others. Be like newborn babies who are thirsty for the pure spiritual milk that will help you grow and be saved… Come to Jesus Christ. He is the living stone that people have rejected, but which God has chosen and highly honoured. And now you are living stones that are being used to build a spiritual house… You are followers of the Lord, and that stone is precious to you. But it isn't precious to those who refuse to follow him. They are the builders who tossed aside the stone that turned out to be the most important one of all.

 Prayer

Dear God, thank you for loving us so much. Help us to know that you love us, even when we feel hurt, alone and afraid. Help us to grow stronger and closer to you. Amen

 Songs

God is so good (KS)
Have you got an appetite? (KS)
Kumbaya (JP)
Make me a channel of your peace (JP)

 Visual aids

❖ A toolbox with a selection of tools including a large hammer, a chisel, a screwdriver, a pair of pliers, a rasp or 'rat-tailed' file, and a large sheet of rough-grade sandpaper.
❖ Alternatively, or preferably in addition, pictures of the characters to show or project.
❖ Some of the children could be encouraged to touch the file and the sandpaper and describe how they feel.

 Main themes

Suffering and personal growth.

Further topics covered

Lent, character development, discipline and discipleship.

FOLLOW-UP

The issue of suffering is a difficult one for adults, let alone young children. Invite the children to talk about a time when they had to do something they didn't like. Issues might include a trip to the dentist, a lesson or subject they didn't like or even a telling-off from the teacher. Encourage them to share how it felt at the time and then if they felt any better afterwards.

It is worth taking a bit of time to draw out the value of going through things that seem unpleasant while they're happening. You could close the session by looking at items in nature that develop though 'suffering'—the apple that ripens in the dark, the coal that becomes a diamond under pressure, and the oyster that produces a pearl by irritation. You could show an apple, a piece of coal and an oyster as illustrations and leave the children to draw pictures of them alongside pictures of Reggie, Ritchie and the other tools.

Once upon a time, not so long ago, in a shed at the bottom of the garden, was a toolbox. I don't know its name but it was big and it was strong and it had many tools inside it. It belonged to the Master Builder, and he loved it and all the tools inside it.

Four of the tools were particularly important. They were good friends who did a lot of work together. Let's meet them, shall we?

(As you introduce the four main characters, you can take them out of the toolbox and/or show them on the screen.)

First, there was Billy the Big Hammer. He was strong and liked working but was inclined to be a bit hard-headed. He was a lot bigger than Sally the Small Hammer, who was only used for the smaller and more delicate jobs. Next there was Clara the Chisel. She was tall and slim but also had rather a sharp tongue. After her came Sammy the Screwdriver. He could turn himself to most jobs and was particularly useful at getting in and out of scrapes. Finally, there was Paula the Pliers. Although she was rather short and fat, once she got a grip on something she never let go!

One fine morning, the four friends were all sitting on the workbench in the Master Builder's shed, waiting for the day's activities to start. 'The Master is making something really special today,' said Billy the Big Hammer, 'Oily Fred told me.'

'Oh, yes, I know,' said Clara the Chisel, who seemed to know everything. 'He's making a statue!'

'What?' said Billy and Sammy together.

'A statue, a statue!' replied Clara sharply.

'Sorry,' said Sammy the Screwdriver,

'I didn't understand that because you sneezed.' 'A STATUE!' shouted Clara.

'There you go again,' said Billy. 'Do you want to borrow my hanky?'

'I'm not sneezing!' shouted Clara again. 'The Master is making a… statue. It's a kind of shape. It's very difficult to do and needs some special tools. Like me,' she added proudly.

'Ooo, I hope he uses me,' cried Paula. 'I'd just love to help him make an achoo!'

'Statue, for the last time,' said Clara. 'It's called a statue.'

'S'right!' called out an unfamiliar gravelly voice from the depths of the big toolbox behind them. 'But you won't be the ones to do it. This is specialist stuff, right? Me 'n' Reg are the boys for this, got it?' And with that, two very rough-looking characters jumped down from the toolbox.

The first was a long dark pointed tool with a wooden handle and very rough sides all round. 'Ritchie's the name,' he said. 'Ritchie Rasp. And this is my mate Reg… Reggie Rough the Leveller, we call 'im. 'E don't say much but 'e gets the job done!'

He pointed to his companion, a large sheet of golden card covered with thousands of what looked like tiny pieces of shining glass.

'Move over, chisel,' grated Ritchie as he pushed past Clara towards the edge of the bench. For once, Clara was silent, and even Billy the Big Hammer looked scared as Ritchie Rasp and Reggie Rough shouldered their way through.

'Ow, that hurt,' cried Paula as Reggie's rough sides scraped down her long green legs.

'Ooo, ouch!' complained Sammy as Reggie Rough rubbed against his long flat nose.

But Reggie Rough the Leveller didn't say a word and didn't seem to care a bit how much he hurt the other tools.

'Never mind,' whispered Clara to the others. 'When the Master comes, he'll tell those two off! He won't use *them* to make his statue, you'll see!'

But when the Master Builder arrived to make his statue, he smiled lovingly at the four friends, then laid them all gently back in the toolbox, where they lay quietly puzzled, listening to the sounds of the Master using Ritchie and Reg to make his statue.

That night, Oily Fred came to them in the dark and soothed their grazed sides and sore bodies with his clear healing oil.

'Oi know 'tis hard to understand, my dears,' he explained in his funny squeaky voice, 'but sometimes, the Master doesn't use us. He puts us on one side and we have to wait. And sometimes he uses people and things we don't like to get his work done. And

sometimes,' said Oily Fred gently as he rubbed his golden oil along Sammy's scratched nose, 'he even lets us get a bit grazed or bruised to help us to grow.'

'But I don't like it,' complained Paula. 'How can it help us grow?'

'It's called discipline,' said Oily Fred. 'Sometimes, we have to go through things that hurt us so that we can learn patience and kindness and love. Once upon a time, a long, long while ago, the Master chose to go through something that hurt him very badly indeed to help us to overcome the bad things in our lives.'

'But why did he do that,' said Sammy curiously, 'especially if he didn't have to?'

'Because he loves us,' said Oily Fred softly. 'Because he loves us.'

Reproduced with permission from *Collective Worship Unwrapped* published by BRF 2005 (978 1 84101 371 8) **www.barnabasinschools.org.uk**

The Toolshed Gang:

The Master Builder

Bible link

John 13:1–17

It was before Passover, and Jesus knew that the time had come for him to leave this world and to return to the Father. He had always loved his followers in this world, and he loved them to the very end… So during the meal Jesus got up, removed his outer garment, and wrapped a towel around his waist. He put some water into a large bowl. Then he began washing his disciples' feet and drying them with the towel he was wearing… After Jesus had washed his disciples' feet and had put his outer garment back on, he sat down again. Then he said: Do you understand what I have done? You call me your teacher and Lord, and you should, because that is who I am. And if your Lord and teacher has washed your feet, you should do the same for each other. I have set the example… I tell you for certain that servants are not greater than their master, and messengers are not greater than the one who sent them. You know these things, and God will bless you, if you do them.

 Visual aids

❖ A toolbox with a selection of tools including a large hammer, a chisel, a screwdriver, a pair of pliers and a workman's apron.
❖ Alternatively, or preferably in addition, pictures of the characters to show or project.

> **Be safe:** Be very careful when allowing the children to handle the tools, especially the chisel and the pliers. The chisel should be masked in a case and children should be discouraged from opening and shutting the pliers. Take the opportunity to stress the importance of tools and the dangers of using them improperly.

Main themes

Servanthood and love.

Further topics covered
Leadership, friendship, Easter.

Prayer

Dear Lord, thank you for dying for us so that we can know forgiveness for all the bad things we have thought, said and done. Amen

Songs

From heaven you came (KS)
Jesus, Jesus, here I am (KS)
Lord of the dance (JP)
One more step along the world I go (JP)

FOLLOW-UP

This assembly provides an excellent opportunity to discuss the heart of Christian belief and the meaning of Easter. Does the Master Builder remind you of anyone? Are we like any of the tools in the toolbox? Which tool do you feel most like? Who does Oily Fred remind you of?

Why did Jesus die on a cross? Is it easy to forgive someone who has hurt you? Do you know anyone who has done something for you even though it has hurt them? What is the best way to help other people?

Use some of the above questions either in a circle time format or as part of a discussion.

Once upon a time, not so long ago, in a shed at the bottom of the garden, was a toolbox. I don't know its name but it was big and it was strong and it had many tools inside it. It belonged to the Master Builder, and he loved it and all the tools inside it.

Four of the tools were particularly important. They were good friends who did a lot of work together. Let's meet them, shall we?

(As you introduce the four main characters, you can take them out of the toolbox and/or show them on the screen.)

First, there was Billy the Big Hammer. He was strong and liked working but was inclined to be a bit hard-headed. He was a lot bigger than Sally the Small Hammer, who was only used for the smaller and more delicate jobs. Next there was Clara the Chisel. She was tall and slim but also had rather a sharp tongue. After her came Sammy the Screwdriver. He could turn himself to most jobs and was particularly useful at getting in and out of scrapes. Finally, there was Paula the Pliers. Although she was

rather short and fat, once she got a grip on something she never let go!

One evening, towards the end of the day, the four friends were all together on the workbench, tired out from the day's labours.

'Phew, have I worked hard today!' panted Billy the Big Hammer. 'The Master had such a lot of hammering to do, I'm completely worn out!'

'Hrrmmpp!' snorted Clara the Chisel with her sharp tongue. 'You think you're tired! I'm absolutely exhausted. I should think I must have made more holes in more pieces of wood than ever before. It's not fair that the Master makes me work so hard!'

'Well, I'm so tired, I don't think I could screw in another screw,' complained Sammy the Screwdriver. 'My nose is sore and my body is aching. The Master just doesn't realize how hard it is working all day!'

Paula the Pliers just lay on her back and groaned. 'Oh, my legs!' she moaned. 'Oh, my poor aching mouth. Do you know how many nails I had to pull out today?' she whined. 'Do you?'

Reproduced with permission from *Collective Worship Unwrapped* published by BRF 2005 (978 1 84101 371 8) www.barnabasinschools.org.uk

So the tools went on complaining and moaning, over and over again. They complained about how tired they felt. They moaned about their aches and pains. Then they started to wonder whether the Master Builder really cared about them at all. They made so much noise that they woke up most of the other tools in the toolbox, who began climbing out to see what all the fuss was about.

(At this point you could introduce a number of other tools, depending on how many you have available. It's probably not a good idea to interrupt the flow of the story by getting other children out to hold them, but they could be shown by you at the front.)

'The Master doesn't really love us at all,' suggested Clara. 'He makes us all work far too hard!'

'If he loved us,' said Sammy bitterly, 'he'd understand how we felt!'

'What does he know about wood and nails, anyway?' said Billy. 'It's not fair!'

'You know what?' said Paula, jumping up on her little green legs. 'I think we should all go on strike! We'll stop working, then the Master will know how we really feel and start giving us a bit more attention!'

'Yeah!!' yelled all the tools together.

All, that is, except one. 'You're all bonkers,' said a funny wheezy voice from the top of the toolbox. 'You really think the Master Builder doesn't love you?'

All the tools looked up, and there stood dirty old Oily Fred, with his '3-in-one' sign just visible on his grubby metal side. 'Paula Pliers, I'm surprised at you,' said Fred. 'Your great-great-grandfather Peter would be ashamed to hear you say what you just said. And after all the Master went through for you! You know very well what Peter did all those years ago.'

'What did Grandpa Peter do for the Master, Paula?' said Timmy the Tilecutter in his high-pitched voice. Paula just hung her head in shame.

'He was called Peter Pincer in those days,' explained Oily Fred, 'and he pulled a huge big nail out of the Master's own hand.'

'Why did he have a nail through his hand?' asked Billy. 'Did he make a mistake?'

'The Master has never made a mistake,' said Fred. 'He had a nail in his hand because he had been killed! Don't you know the story?'

And so, while all the tools gathered around the toolbox to listen, Oily Fred told them about how the Master Builder's love for them all had led to his death.

'He died so that all the bad things you do and say can be forgiven,' said Fred, 'but the good news is that he came alive again and lives and works for us every day. He is our Master but he also works as our servant and friend. That's why he wears that big apron every day. He calls it his Servant Apron.'

'I didn't know that,' said Clara quietly. 'I thought the apron was so that he wouldn't get messy when we're working for him.'

'Oh no,' said Oily Fred as he smiled down at all the assembled tools. 'The Master Builder gave himself for all of us, and he still gives himself every day. He loves us more than we can imagine, and his love for us will last for ever!'

Reproduced with permission from *Collective Worship Unwrapped* published by BRF 2005 (978 1 84101 371 8) www.barnabasinschools.org.uk

Honky the Donkey

Bible link

Luke 10:25–37

As a man was going down from Jerusalem to Jericho, robbers attacked him and grabbed everything he had. They beat him up and ran off, leaving him half dead.

A priest happened to be going down the same road. But when he saw the man, he walked by on the other side. Later a temple helper came to the same place. But when he saw the man who had been beaten up, he also went by on the other side. A man from Samaria then came travelling along that road. When he saw the man, he felt sorry for him and went over to him. He treated his wounds with olive oil and wine and bandaged them. Then he put him on his own donkey and took him to an inn, where he took care of him…

Then Jesus asked, 'Which one of these three people was a real neighbour to the man who was beaten up by robbers?'

Visual aids

❖ A donkey: this can be a balloon donkey (see p. 128 for suggested suppliers), a toy donkey or even a picture on an OHP (see p. 124).

❖ You could ask an adult to look after the donkey and afterwards give it to the child who has listened especially hard.

Explain that Jesus told a story a bit like this in the Bible. Updating the parable with references to cheese-and-pickle sandwiches and visits to McDonald's ground the narrative in the contemporary world. However, do maintain integrity by explaining that this is a modern-day version of the Bible story.

The 'Yo! Henry' technique keeps the attention focused, as the children are waiting for the word to come up. Changes of voice add dimension to characters. Small bits of costume are also useful—hats, spectacles, scarves, shawls and so on.

The humour in the story detracts attention slightly from the violence and the serious nature of mugging. However, gently dissuade the children from laughing at the attack on Henry (*Yo! Henry!*) by pointing out that it really wasn't very nice.

Main themes

Prejudice and friendship.

Further topics covered
Racism, difference, helping others.

Prayer

Thank you, God, for our friends. Help us to be a good friend to people who are different from us. Show us that the best way to make friends is to be one ourselves. Amen

Songs

Bind us together, Lord (JP)
Have you seen the pussycat? (KS)
Thank you for my friends (TB)

You could end the story by talking about people who are different from us (people who look, behave or speak differently) and how important it is to care even when they are different. If appropriate, this could move into a discussion of prejudice and how we handle it, with particular reference to school policies in this area.

Once… upon a… time… there was… a man… called… Henry! What was he called? *(Henry)* Every time you hear his name, say, 'Yo! Henry!' *(wag your finger)*

Now Henry *(Yo! Henry!)* was a nice man. He was a kind man. He was a gentle man. He had lots of friends in his little village. There was the vicar—the Reverend Harty Larfer. There was the nice lady who kept the corner shop— Mrs Helen Highwater. And many others. Oh yes, Henry *(Yo! Henry!)* had lots of friends.

But there was one person he didn't like. Oh yes, Sam! He was so rude to poor Sam. He talked behind his back. He called him bad names. He even said, 'You smell!' Oooo! And all because of Sam's pet donkey, Honky.

All night long, Honky kept Henry *(Yo! Henry!)* awake with his braying. Heeee haaaawww! Heeee haaawww!! Heeee haaawww!!! Such a terrible noise! Honky the Donkey was so noisy. And he could eat anything. One day he got into Henry's *(Yo! Henry!)* garden and ate his washing! Heeeeeee haaaaawwww!

One fine day, Henry *(Yo! Henry!)* had to go on a long journey. There were no buses or trains or cars in those days, so he had to go on foot. He put on his strong walking boots and his smart casual jacket, packed up his favourite sandwiches—cheese and pickle—and set off. The sun was shining brightly, the sky was blue—it was a lovely day for a journey.

Unfortunately, it didn't stay lovely. Oh no! For hiding behind some rocks along the way were three very unpleasant robbers. I'll tell you their names. They were Bugsy, Mugsy and Thugsy! *(You could use three different voices for these characters, or three different hats.)*

The three robbers jumped out on poor Henry *(Yo! Henry!)*. Bugsy punched him on the nose. Mugsy thumped him in the stomach. Thugsy stamped on his foot. (It's not funny! That's really horrid!) They tore his nice jacket, they stole all his money, and they even ate his cheese and pickle sandwiches! Finally, they pushed him into a deep hole by the side of the road and ran off laughing. Ha ha ha! He he he! Ho ho ho! *(Use three voices or hats again)* Poor Henry *(Yo! Henry!)*

Henry just lay in the bottom of the hole, feeling very sad. His head ached, his tummy was sore and he'd lost one of his shoes. He called out, 'Help! Help me, please, somebody! M-m-my name's Henry *(Yo! Henry!)* and I'm stuck in this hole. Help!'

Just then, he heard the sound of footsteps coming down the road, and a voice singing *(something suitably clerical)*. A head

Reproduced with permission from *Collective Worship Unwrapped* published by BRF 2005 (978 1 84101 371 8) **www.barnabasinschools.org.uk**

appeared at the top of the hole and looked down at him. It was the vicar, the Reverend Harty Larfer. Thank goodness!

'Oh, Vicar, I'm so pleased to see you. I've been attacked by robbers and they've taken my money and eaten my…'

'Robbers? Robbers! Oh, my goodness me,' said the vicar. 'I don't like robbers! Er, look, I've just remembered—I'm late for the morning service. Sorry. Must dash. Sorry. Bye!'

And with that, the vicar disappeared! Poor Henry. *(Yo! Henry!)* He called out even louder: 'Help! Help me, please, somebody! M-m-my name's Henry. *(Yo! Henry!)* and I'm stuck in this hole.'

Just then, he heard the sound of footsteps coming down the road, and someone whistling *(I love to go a-wandering, English country garden or something similar)*. A head appeared at the top of the hole and looked down at him. It was Mrs Highwater, the nice lady from the corner shop. Thank goodness!

'Oh, Helen, I'm so pleased to see you. I've been attacked by robbers, and they've taken my money and eaten my sandwiches and I'm dirty and my nose is bleeding and I've lost my…'

'Dirt? Blood! O dear me, no! I can't stand blood. I've got my best frock on. I just couldn't get that dirty. So sorry. Really must go. Sorry. Bye!'

And with that, Helen disappeared! Poor Henry. *(Yo! Henry!)* He started to cry. He called out even louder still: 'Help! Help me, please, somebody! M-m-my name's Henry *(Yo! Henry!)* and I'm stuck in this hole.'

Once more, he heard the sound of footsteps coming down the road—big heavy footsteps. Another head appeared at the top of the hole and looked down at him. Then he heard a terrible sound… Heeeee haaaawww!! Oh no! Honky the Donkey!

Poor Henry *(Yo! Henry!)* Now he was in real trouble. It was his worst enemy!

Suddenly the end of a rope dropped down the side of the hole and a voice called out: 'Grab hold! I'll pull you out!'

Sam! Well, well. Quick as a flash, Henry *(Yo! Henry!)* was out of the hole and a kind and smiling Sam was helping him. Sam brushed off his jacket, found his missing shoe, dabbed his poorly nose with a hanky and gave him some orange juice to drink. Then… he helped him carefully on to the back of… Honky the Donkey! The donkey didn't seem to mind at all and was really still and quiet.

A little further down the road, they came to a McDonald's. Sam took Henry *(Yo! Henry!)* in and bought him a Big Mac and fries (supersized) and a Coke. 'And if you're still hungry afterwards,' he said, 'you can have a Macflurry!'

Henry *(Yo! Henry!)* and Sam talked and talked. They both discovered how easy it is to make friends. Sam became Henry's *(Yo! Henry!)* best friend. And Henry *(Yo! Henry!)* even came to like… Honky the Donkey!

Big Bad Brian the Lion

Telling a story from an unusual angle

 Bible link

Daniel 6:16–28

Darius ordered Daniel to be… thrown into a pit of lions… A stone was rolled over the pit, and it was sealed. Then Darius and his officials stamped the seal to show that no one should let Daniel out. All night long the king could not sleep… At daybreak the king got up and ran to the pit. He was anxious and shouted, 'Daniel, you were faithful and served your God. Was he able to save you from the lions?' Daniel answered, 'Your Majesty… My God knew that I was innocent, and he sent an angel to keep the lions from eating me…' The king was relieved to hear Daniel's voice, and he gave orders for him to be taken out of the pit. Daniel's faith in his God had kept him from being harmed…

FOLLOW-UP

After the story, ask questions like 'What was the name of the man in the corner? Where can we find his story? Do you think he was frightened?' (Stress the fact that God doesn't always take away our fear but helps us cope with it. Real bravery is carrying on even when we are afraid.)

What things are you afraid of? Suggest a few—creepy crawlies, the dark, bullies and so on. Use this to lead into talking about bullies, if appropriate, and encourage children to talk to God, and tell their parents, teachers or an adult they trust, about any instances of bullying.

This is a good session to follow up with class work or circle time.

King Darius then sent this message to all people of every nation and race in the world: '… I command everyone in my kingdom to worship and honour the God of Daniel. He is the living God, the one who lives for ever.'

 Visual aids

❖ A lion. Use a balloon lion (see the resource section for suggested suppliers), a toy lion or the picture on page 125.
❖ You could ask an adult to look after the lion and afterwards give it to someone in the school considered especially brave.

Involve the children, with lots of faces, voices, changes of pace and volume.

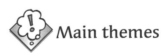 Main themes

Bullying and courage.

Further topics covered
Fear, protection, prayer.

 Prayer

Dear God, please be with us when we feel scared. Thank you for sending your angel to protect Daniel in the den of lions. Help us to trust you even when we are afraid. Amen

 Songs

Be bold, be strong! (KS)
I'm not alone, for my Father is with me (SFK)
There once was a man called Daniel (KS)
Who's the king of the jungle? (KS)

Once upon a time, there was a lion. He was called Brian. He was very big and very strong and… and he was a bully! He thought he was bigger and better than any of the other animals in the jungle. Everywhere he went, he boasted about how clever and how strong he was. 'I'm big bad Brian the Lion!' he would snarl at anyone he met. 'RRROOOAAARRR!!!' And he showed all his huge teeth and his huge claws and his huge orange lion's mane.

The other animals were scared of him. I don't blame them, do you?

For instance, one day, Mr Giraffe was quietly minding his own business, chomping away at the sweetest, tenderest leaves on the topmost branches of the trees. Big bad Brian the lion crept up behind him so softly, so quietly, and then…

'I'm big bad Brian the Lion! RRROOOAAARRR!!!'

Poor Mr Giraffe! He was scared out of his skin and ran off into the jungle. Brian just laughed.

For instance, one day, Mrs Elephant was quietly minding her own business, having a nice cool mud bath at the edge of the river. Big bad Brian the lion crept up behind her so softly, so quietly, and then…

'I'm big bad Brian the Lion! RRROOOAAARRR!!!'

Poor Mrs Elephant! She was scared out of her skin and ran off into the jungle. Brian just laughed.

For instance, one day, Mr Monkey was quietly minding his own business, chomping away at a banana, peeling down the firm yellow skin to enjoy the soft white middle. Big bad Brian the lion crept up behind him so softly, so quietly, and then…

'I'm big bad Brian the Lion! RRROOOAAARRR!!!'

Poor Mr Monkey! He was scared out of his skin and ran off into the jungle. Brian just laughed.

What a rotten bully!

Now, one day, Brian was swaggering

Reproduced with permission from *Collective Worship Unwrapped* published by BRF 2005 (978 1 84101 371 8) www.barnabasinschools.org.uk

through the jungle, thinking how big and strong and clever he was, when suddenly… a huge net dropped out of the trees right on top of him, and several fierce-looking men with spears jumped out from behind the bushes. Brian snarled and roared and struggled and rolled, but he couldn't get free. The fierce men bundled Brian into a large bamboo cage on wheels and pushed him down the jungle trail. Before long, they came to a wide road that led them to a huge walled city, and Brian's cage was wheeled through the open gates. People on each side jeered at Brian and threw stones and rotten fruit at him. He growled and snarled and scratched but he couldn't reach any of them. In the middle of the city, the cage was pushed up to the edge of a great hole in the ground and Brian was suddenly tipped in!

It was dark and dusty at the bottom of the hole, and there were several other lions down there, but Brian was bigger and fiercer than any of them and they soon backed off. When his eyes grew used to the gloom, Brian saw a man sitting in a far corner of the hole. He had his back to Brian and his hands clasped together. He seemed to be muttering something under his breath. Here was Brian's chance to really frighten someone! Big bad Brian the lion crept up behind the man so softly, so quietly, and then…

'I'm big bad Brian the Lion! RRROOOAAARRR!!!'

The man didn't move! He didn't seem to notice Brian at all, and just kept on muttering, his head on his chest. Brian was puzzled. This had never happened before. He took a deep breath and growled even louder.

'I'm big bad Brian the Lion! RRROOOAAARRR!!!'

The man still didn't move!! He just kept on talking quietly under his breath, his head bowed and his hands clasped tightly together. Brian took a huge deep breath. His eyes bulged! His great fangs stretched wide!! His huge black lion's mane stuck straight out from his head, making him look twice as big!!!

'I'm big bad Brian the Lion! RRROOOAAARRR!!!'

The man still didn't move!!! Suddenly, something tapped Brian on the shoulder. He turned round and found himself facing a gigantic figure over ten feet tall, all dressed in shining white with massive golden wings.

'MY NAME'S GABRIEL AND I'M AN ANGEL!!!'

Poor Brian! He was scared out of his skin and ran whimpering into the corner like a frightened little kitten.

And do you know what? I think it served him right!

Reproduced with permission from *Collective Worship Unwrapped* published by BRF 2005 (978 1 84101 371 8) www.barnabasinschools.org.uk

Mr Silver's guest

A version of this story appeared in *Luke's Thrilling Gospel* by Ivor Powell, who himself quoted from the stories of Dr Frank Boreham.

Bible link

Luke 11:1–13

Suppose one of you goes to a friend in the middle of the night and says, 'Let me borrow three loaves of bread. A friend of mine has dropped in, and I don't have a thing for him to eat.' And suppose your friend answers, 'Don't bother me! The door is bolted, and my children and I are in bed. I cannot get up to give you something.' He may not get up and give you the bread, just because you are his friend. But he will get up and give you as much as you need, simply because you are not ashamed to keep on asking. So I tell you to ask and you will receive, search and you will find, knock and the door will be opened for you. Everyone who asks will receive, everyone who searches will find, and the door will be opened for everyone who knocks.

Visual aids

❖ Some volunteer 'actors' to play Mr Copper, Mr Silver, Mrs Silver, Mr Gold and Mr Gold's family (wife and children).
❖ Some props and dressing-up costumes (hats, jackets and so on).
❖ A reindeer: here again you can use a balloon (see the resource section) or a toy or picture.

You don't have to pick boys to play male parts and girls to play female parts. It is just as much fun to have, say, Mr Copper, Mr Silver and Mr Gold played by girls. This is true for most assemblies involving Key Stage One and Two, although care should be taken with older children.

This assembly depends on two important aspects of storytelling—audience participation and a 'tag-line' that you've encouraged the children to listen for.

Main themes

Prayer and persistence.

Further topics covered
Hospitality, grace, mission.

Prayer

Thank you, Lord, for teaching us to pray and never give up. Thank you for listening to us when we talk to you and for helping us to help our friends. Amen

Songs

Ask! Ask! Ask! (JP)
Oh, oh, oh, how good is the Lord (KS)
Prayer is like a telephone (KS)
What a friend we have in Jesus (JP)

FOLLOW-UP

Talk about friends and what we might be prepared to do for them. Invite responses from those willing to say how far they have been prepared to go to help their friends. Encourage a discussion on what prayer might be. Is it just asking God for what we want? Do we think God will give us whatever we ask for? Are you ever tempted to give up on something you've been trying for a long time?

You could conclude by briefly affirming that God is far more ready to listen than we are to pray, that he is always ready to hear our prayers and we should never give up talking to him even if it seems like he hasn't heard.

Once upon a time, there was a kind man called Mr Silver. He lived with his wife in a little house on the edge of the town.

(By the way… there's a reindeer in this story in a very unexpected place, so I want you all to listen ever so carefully. If you can spot when the reindeer turns up in the story, don't shout out, don't make a noise. Just put your hand straight up and wait until I ask you.)

Now, where was I? Ah, yes… Mr Silver and his wife and their pet rrr… rrr… rrrabbit lived in a little house on the edge of town. They were very happy and had lots of friends. But their best friend was Mr Gold. Mr Gold and his family lived in a very splendid house with a large front door with a big brass handle right in the middle of the town. Mr Gold was the kindest, gentlest and nicest man in town, and Mr Silver knew that if he ever needed anything he could always go to his best friend, Mr Gold.

(By the way… I'm sure we could imagine this story a lot better if we had some volunteers to play the main parts)

(Organize this with help from the teaching staff, and dress the children accordingly.)

Now, one evening, when it was quite late, Mr Silver and his wife were just getting ready for bed. He was just checking the rabbit hutch to make sure Flopsy had enough to eat and drink when he looked up and saw a familiar figure walking down the road to meet him. The visitor looked very tired, as if he had been travelling a long while, and behind him was a rrr… rrr… rrrucksack carried on his back. It was Mr Copper, Mr Silver's oldest friend, come for an unexpected visit.

'Mr Copper, my old friend,' said Mr Silver. 'Welcome! You look as if you've been travelling for a long time and could do with a rest and a bite of something to eat. Come in, come in!' He took Mr Copper's heavy rucksack and sat him down at the kitchen table. 'Look who's here,' he said to his wife. 'Could you get something for Mr Copper's supper? I bet he's really hungry. Can we get you a meal, Mr Copper? Perhaps a rrr… a rrr… a rrroast dinner?'

'Don't go to any trouble,' replied Mr Copper. 'A cup of tea would be lovely, and, possibly… a couple of cheese and pickle sandwiches?'

'No trouble at all, old friend,' said Mr Silver. 'Do you mind getting us all a spot of supper, dear?' he said to his wife.

Mrs Silver went to the larder cupboard and fetched the tea, milk and sugar and a large piece of cheese. She also took down the pickle jar, full of rich spicy pickle! But when

Reproduced with permission from *Collective Worship Unwrapped* published by BRF 2005 (978 1 84101 371 8) www.barnabasinschools.org.uk

she opened the bread bin, there was not a loaf to be found. Not a slice. Not even a crumb! She called Mr Silver over and whispered in his ear, 'We've got no bread!'

Poor Mr Copper! He was as hungry as a rrr… as hungry as a rrr… as hungry as a rrrhinoceros! But there would be no sandwiches for him unless Mr Silver could come up with an answer. 'I know!' said Mrs Silver. 'Why don't you call on your friend, Mr Gold? He's bound to have some bread!'

Mr Silver's eyes lit up and, pulling on his overcoat, he slipped out of the front door and made his way down the street to Mr Gold's house. It was quite dark by now and most of the bedroom lights in the houses were out.

Meanwhile, at Mr Gold's house, Mr and Mrs Gold were getting ready for bed themselves. Both the children were already asleep (pause for the snores!), Mrs Gold was putting out the lights and Mr Gold was pulling the front-room curtains.

'Hmmmm,' said Mr Gold as he glanced out the window, 'it sure looks like rain, dear.' (Reindeer—wait for the hands, or groans, and respond appropriately.) Mr and Mrs Gold trudged up the stairs, climbed into bed and were soon fast asleep. Time passed… then…

BANG, BANG, BANG! There came a loud knocking on Mr Gold's large front door with the big brass handle. Yes, you've guessed—it was Mr Silver! 'Hello, hello?' he shouted through the letterbox. 'It's me—your friend, Mr Silver!' No answer…

BANG, BANG, BANG! Still no answer. BANG, BANG, BANG! 'Hello, are you there? Mr Gold? It's Mr Silver! My old friend, Mr Copper, has just arrived late and we've got no

bread to make him a sandwich. Have you got any bread? … Please? … Mr Gold!'

Finally, Mr Gold woke up. 'Come back tomorrow,' he called. 'We're all asleep in bed and it's very late!'

BANG, BANG, BANG! 'Please, Mr Gold, please! Just one loaf, that's all I want!'

Well, this conversation could have gone on all night, but finally Mr Gold got up and very sleepily pulled on his slippers and dressing-gown. He trudged downstairs and got a large crusty brown loaf from the bread bin and took it to Mr Silver on the doorstep. 'There you are, my friend,' he yawned. 'Good night.'

Mr Silver ran back home through the dark streets and before too long he and his wife and Mr Copper were all sitting down to a steaming pot of tea and a large plate of delicious cheese and pickle sandwiches. What a great time they had!

Reproduced with permission from *Collective Worship Unwrapped* published by BRF 2005 (978 1 84101 371 8) www.barnabasinschools.org.uk

Bubbles

STORYTELLING METHOD

Using a visual aid as a tool for reflection

Bible link

1 Corinthians 15:50–58

My friends, I want you to know that our bodies of flesh and blood will decay. This means that they cannot share in God's kingdom, which lasts for ever. I will explain a mystery to you. Not every one of us will die, but we will all be changed. It will happen suddenly, quicker than the blink of an eye. At the sound of the last trumpet the dead will be raised. We will all be changed, so that we will never die again. Our dead and decaying bodies will be changed into bodies that won't die or decay. The bodies we now have are weak and can die. But they will be changed into bodies that are eternal. Then the Scriptures will come true, 'Death has lost the battle! Where is its victory? Where is its sting?'

Visual aids

❖ A tub of dilute washing-up liquid (for bubbles) and a bubble blower.

FOLLOW-UP

Make a list or chart setting out the lifespan of persons, places and things. Share some information about record timespans and lifespans. Discuss how things get old and wear out. Be prepared to discuss specific items, possessions and so on. Ask if anyone has been to a funeral and what it felt like.

This would be a good opportunity for a circle time to discuss our attitudes to and feelings about death, separation and grief. How do we know that love lasts for ever? Why is God's love so special?

❖ Optional extra: a large red heart cushion. (You may be able to obtain this from a department store.)

Helpful hints

It is always best to get real bubble mixture from a toy shop or confectioner. Be careful with very small children in the unlikely event of bubbles popping in eyes. Note: a well-lit hall or one that has coloured lights could produce some wonderful reflections on the bubbles.

There are some excellent books for children on the subject of death and bereavement. My favourites are listed in the resources section at the back of this book.

Main themes

Death and change.

Further topics covered

Bereavement, love, growing older.

Prayer

Dear God, thank you that your love never wears out or fades away. Help us to know that everlasting love deep inside. May that love comfort us when we are sad or lonely. Thank you, God. Amen

Songs

God's love is like a circle (see page 128)
Jesus, Jesus, here I am (KS)
Kumbaya (JP)
The steadfast love of the Lord (JP)

Begin by sitting quietly and blowing some bubbles. Encourage the children to sit quietly and watch the bubbles rather than jumping up to pop them. Try to blow the bubbles away from where the children are sitting. Remark on how beautiful the bubbles are and how prettily they catch the light. The only problem is that they don't seem to last very long!

Get one of the teachers to choose (one by one) six or so children to participate in a bubble-blowing competition. You could see who can make the largest bubble or, better still, the longest lasting. It is more fun if you encourage everyone to count as the bubble floats through the air. Just be sure that, each time, the children count at the same speed. Give a little prize to the winner. Ideally this should be given to the child's teacher for safe keeping, to be returned at the end of the school day.

Comment again on how the bubbles don't seem to last very long, although they are extremely beautiful while they do. Can anyone think of other things that don't last very long? (You can make suggestions of your own, even illustrating with visual examples, if you wish.) Sweets don't last long, especially scrummy ones! Burgers and pizzas last… how long? Five minutes? Ten? Ice-creams don't last very long if it's hot and sunny. Puddles don't last because they dry up, and kittens and puppies don't stay small for long. They soon become cats and dogs! Can you think of anything else that doesn't last long? Holidays? Playtime? Football matches? Cartoons? Roast dinners? (Get the children to put their hands up with suggestions.)

What can you think of that does last for a long time? Schools? Buildings? Churches? Houses? (Get the children to put their hands up with further suggestions.)

Hmmm. It seems like nothing lasts for ever, does it? What about people? Boys and girls and men and women? We all get older, don't we? We grow and we change. Boys grow into men, and girls grow into women. Children don't last—they turn into grown-ups! But men and women don't last for ever either, do they? They get older and older, and then they wear out altogether and they die.

(You may now need to give some time for children to say if they have a relative who has died, or even—quite possibly—a pet. This will, of course, need to be handled carefully and sensitively but you may well find that the children are a lot more comfortable talking about death than you are.)

Death is something that happens to everyone, sometime or another. Now and then, someone dies who is quite young, and that is very sad.

They may have an accident or an illness. Most people die when they get very old and come to the end of their lives. This is sad too.

Well, it seems as if nothing lasts for ever. Everything wears out or dies. Those lovely bubbles were bright and beautiful but they didn't last very long, did they? We all last longer than soap bubbles, but we still don't last for ever. Can you think of anything that lasts for ever; something that just goes on and on and never dies? Here's a clue to help you guess.

(Produce the heart cushion or something similar, and encourage hands to go up.)

Love! That goes on for ever. And the best love of all is God's love! That never wears out and never dies. God says that if his true love is in our hearts, we can go on for ever too! When we die, he'll give us a new indestructible body and a new life that will go on and on and on and on and on and on and on and on and…! Now, that's a love worth having, isn't it?

Reproduced with permission from *Collective Worship Unwrapped* published by BRF 2005 (978 1 84101 371 8) **www.barnabasinschools.org.uk**

The little yellow line

Bible link

Luke 2:1–20

Mary was engaged to Joseph and travelled with him to Bethlehem. She was soon going to have a baby, and while they were there, she gave birth to her firstborn son. She dressed him in baby clothes and laid him on a bed of hay, because there was no room for them in the inn. That night in the fields near Bethlehem some shepherds were guarding their sheep. All at once an angel came down to them from the Lord, and the brightness of the Lord's glory flashed around them. The shepherds were frightened. But the angel said, 'Don't be afraid! I have good news for you… This very day in King David's home town a Saviour was born for you. He is Christ the Lord. You will know who he is, because you will find him dressed in baby clothes and lying on a bed of hay.' … After the angels had left and gone back to heaven, the shepherds said to each other, 'Let's go to Bethlehem and see what the Lord has told us about.' They hurried off and found Mary and Joseph, and they saw the baby lying on a bed of hay.

Visual aids

❖ A bright yellow latex modelling balloon (see the resource section for suggested suppliers).

Helpful hints

Blow the balloon up with a pump if your lungs can't take the strain. Remember to leave a little space at the 'nipple end' and let a little air out of the 'nozzle end' before tying off. The squeezing and twisting of the balloon throughout the story are essential to the final product. If the balloon modelling is beyond you, try an alternative, such as a large yellow pipe cleaner or a piece of bendable yellow wire.

This is a particularly good assembly for very young children.

Main themes

Christmas and being special.

Further topics covered

Self-esteem, helping others.

Prayer

Thank you, Lord God, for all the people whose jobs we easily overlook. Thank you for making them special. And thank you for sending Jesus to us at Christmas to remind us that we are special too. Amen

Songs

I'm special (KS)
Jesus bids us shine (JP)
O little town of Bethlehem (JP)

Have a discussion about people and objects that nobody notices. Ask for examples, and tell them some of your own. How does it feel to be overlooked and unnoticed? How can we know that we are special? How can we help other people to feel special?

Once upon a time, there was a little yellow line. Now you all know what job yellow lines have, don't you? That's right… they lie at the edge of the road to remind people not to park there. Sometimes there are two of them side by side and we call them a double yellow line. Woe betide you if you park there! I don't expect any of your mums and dads would dream of doing that, would they? No, of course not! Anyway… back to the story.

The little yellow line lay by the side of a road that led to a little town nearby. Day after day he lay there, letting people know, 'You can't park here!' I don't suppose many people noticed him lying there. After all, how many of us take any notice of the little yellow lines by the roadside in *our* town? But he noticed *them*. Tall people and short people, young and old. Boys and girls playing ball and shouting to each other. People in a hurry and people with time to spare. They all passed him on their way to the nearby town.

As time went by, the little yellow line began to get bored of doing the same thing all day, just lying at the roadside without moving. He longed to have an adventure, to do something interesting for a change. And so it happened…

One evening, he was lying, wondering if he'd ever do anything different, when he spotted a couple approaching him along the road. It was a man and a woman. The man looked very anxious and the woman looked very tired. She was riding a donkey. Something about this couple made the little yellow line sit up and take notice, and as they went by he made up his mind. He pulled himself up off the road and followed them into the town.

Before long, the couple came to a ramshackle old shed and pushed inside. The little yellow line squeezed in after them and hid himself behind the door. The little shed was dark and smelly and very crowded. There were two cows, four pigs, half a dozen chickens, three ferrets, 22 mice and a spider! Golly! As the little yellow line looked closer, he realized that the woman was about to have a baby—in a dirty old shed…!

Just then, a gruff old farmer pushed his way into the shed and threw some hay down on the floor for the man and woman. He pushed the door so hard that the little yellow line was squashed into a spring, which went 'booooiiinnnngg' and shot right out of the window, across the road and into a neighbouring field.

Reproduced with permission from *Collective Worship Unwrapped* published by BRF 2005 (978 1 84101 371 8) www.barnabasinschools.org.uk

(Push the balloon into a zigzag shape and mime it shooting across the road.)

The little yellow line lay in the field for a moment, partly stunned. Then he started to look around. Just nearby was a small lamb with its foot stuck in a hole, bleating pitifully. The little yellow line leapt into action, forming himself into a loop *(do this with the balloon)* and throwing himself around the little lamb's neck. He pulled and pulled and finally got the lamb out of the hole. Across the other side of the field he could see the sheep gathering, so he gently pulled the lamb towards them. On the way, he was able to loop himself *(do this with the balloon)* around two other sheep in difficulties and get them all safely back to the flock.

As he lay back, feeling quite tired out by his efforts, he began to hear a wonderful and mysterious sound. It was the music of a most beautiful song, and it filled the air about him. Bright shining figures appeared in the air by the flock, and the music grew louder and louder so that the little yellow line felt he would almost burst from the joy of it. He felt himself getting lighter and lighter, and before he knew it he was floating high above the earth. As he floated, he felt himself changing.

(Twist the balloon into a star shape as illustrated on page 50.)

All of a sudden, the Christmas angel appeared beside him, floating in the air. 'Oh, Christmas angel!' said the little yellow line. 'What's happening to me? I feel so strange.'

'Little yellow line,' said the Christmas angel, 'you are very special. You are helping to make the first Christmas!'

'Who, me?' said the little yellow line. 'But I'm nobody. I'm just a little yellow line that lies in the road that no one notices. How can I be special?'

'You showed Mary and Joseph the way to Bethlehem,' said the angel. 'You helped the lost lambs back to the flock so that they were all ready for the song of the heavenly host. And look, you see those figures down there?' The angel pointed to a group of travellers far below them on the earth. 'If you shine hard enough, you can guide the wise men on their way to the stable where the baby Jesus is to be born. You *are* special, little yellow line— you're a star!'

And the little yellow line—who was now a beautiful shining star—shone and shone and shone!

Reproduced with permission from *Collective Worship Unwrapped* published by BRF 2005 (978 1 84101 371 8) **www.barnabasinschools.org.uk**

HOW TO MAKE A BALLOON STAR

1. Purchase a yellow latex modelling balloon (No. 260Q). Details of suppliers can be found on page 128.

2. Inflate the balloon. To save your lungs it is best to use a balloon pump for this! Leave approximately 7.5cm uninflated (Figure 1).

Figure 1

3. Squeeze the balloon to distribute the air evenly throughout its length and then tie the ends together (Figure 2). This will take up the uninflated 'slack'.

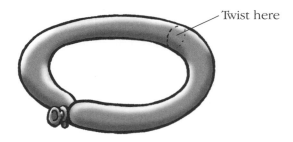

Twist here

Figure 2

4. Pull the two sides of the circle apart and twist the lower half of the circle (Figure 3) so you now have two equal and parallel lengths with a twist at each end.

Twist here   Twist here

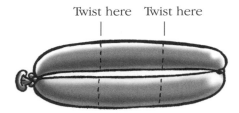

Figure 3

5. Now put two twists evenly spaced along the length of the two halves of the balloon as indicated in Figure 3. Be sure to twist both halves together.

6. Fold the first third under the middle and the last third over the middle as in Figure 4.

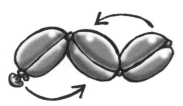

Figure 4

7. Now the difficult bit! You are holding six 15cm sections of balloon all folded on top of each other. Push all the twisted junctions together into the centre and twist the whole thing once more. Voila! A star. (Figure 5)

Figure 5

Key Stage One and Two assemblies

Samson the Superhero

STORYTELLING METHOD

Audience participation

Bible link

Judges 16:15–31

Delilah started nagging and pestering Samson… until he… told her the truth. 'I have belonged to God ever since I was born, so my hair has never been cut. If it were ever cut off, my strength would leave me…' The Philistine rulers went to Delilah's house… Delilah had lulled Samson to sleep with his head resting in her lap. She signalled to one of the Philistine men as she began cutting off Samson's seven braids. And by the time she had finished, Samson's strength was gone.

FOLLOW-UP

This powerful Old Testament story could raise a lot of questions that will need to be handled very sensitively. You could begin by discussing the subject of fighting—from war, through boxing, wrestling and so on, to fights and squabbles in the playground. Encourage the children to think about fighting that might be necessary and fighting that can be avoided. Draw out the point that a lot of the warring and fighting in the Old Testament is a picture of our 'fight' against wrongdoing and evil. Encourage the children to make the distinction between physical and 'spiritual' conflict.

Alternatively, you could discuss the feelings of some of the main characters. How does it feel to be betrayed by someone you trusted? How does it feel to break a promise? How does it feel to let God down?

Visual aids

❖ A couple of pairs of sports socks.
❖ Optional extras: some pictures or slides or videos of modern superheroes, such as Superman, Batman, Spiderman, the Hulk, the X Men and so on.

Helpful hints

This is an assembly that you can put together quickly if need be. The main topic, as you will see below, is 'sex and violence', but this is sex and violence for Key Stages 1 and 2, Bible-style!

Main themes

Sex and violence.

Further topics covered

Power, obedience, trust in God, fighting.

Prayer

Dear God, help us to trust you and never break our promises. Help us to know that you are with us, even in difficult times. Thank you, God. Amen

Songs

Lord, we've come to worship you (SFK)
My God is so big (KS)
So if you think you're standing firm (KS)

Who is your favourite superhero?

(Ask for suggestions from the children and possibly even the teaching staff.)

My favourite is Danger Mouse *(or whoever your favourite superhero is. If you haven't got one, shame on you—make one up!).*

(Find out some of their superheroes' special powers. You could even compare the merits of one superhero against another, or decide which one has the 'coolest' costume. I'm not sure how cool it is to wear your underpants on the outside of your trousers!)

Anyway—I've discovered a dead easy way to turn yourself into a superhero, and all you need is a couple of pairs of old socks. You roll up the socks and stuff them inside the shoulders of your jumper, and it makes your muscles look bigger.

(Do this—you may even get a laugh.)

You could add other socks to make extra muscles, but not too many or your mums will be after me for ruining your clothes!

(This might be the point at which to add that all the flying and zapping and so on that superheroes do at the movies is courtesy of very clever special effects, and that none of us should even dream of copying them. OK, dreaming about it is actually quite nice; just don't try to do it.)

Did you know that there are superheroes in the Bible? Oh yes—and one of the most incredible was Samson. He was as strong as the Hulk and as good-looking as Wolverine. If ever there was a problem, Samson would just flex his mighty muscles and say, 'This is a job… for SAMSON!'

(As you say this, strike a pose and flex your sock-muscles. You could use the audience-participation technique used in the earlier stories here. For example, every time you say the name 'Samson', the children respond, 'Hooray!'; every time you say the name 'Delilah', they respond, 'Oooh, la la!'; and every time you say 'the Philistines', they respond, 'Boo!'

For instance, one night **Samson** was sleeping in a village when his arch-enemies, **the Philistines**, surrounded the place to trap him. But **Samson** got up in the middle of the night while **the Philistines** were sleeping, and marched to the walls. He said, 'This is a job… for **SAMSON**!' Then he lifted the whole gate—gateposts, crosspiece and all—and carried it out on his shoulders and straight up the nearest hill.

For instance, one day he was attacked by a huge roaring lion. 'This is a job… for **SAMSON**!' he shouted, and with one blow he killed the lion.

For instance, one day he was tied up and delivered to **the Philistines** to be made prisoner. He shouted again, 'This is a job… for **SAMSON**!' and with a great jerk he broke all the ropes around him and attacked **the Philistines** single-handed. With only a donkey bone in his hand, he beat one thousand of them!

What a super superhero! Like most

Reproduced with permission from *Collective Worship Unwrapped* published by BRF 2005 (978 1 84101 371 8) www.barnabasinschools.org.uk

superheroes, **Samson** had secret powers, but unlike most superheroes, his superpower came from God. When **Samson** was young, he'd made a promise to God that he would always obey him. **Samson** promised God that he would never cut his hair, as a sign of his loyalty and friendship towards God. In return, God made **Samson** super-strong and a great leader.

The Philistines, **Samson**'s arch-enemies, did everything they could to destroy **Samson**, but they could never find the secret of his great strength or break his trust in God. So, knowing one of **Samson**'s weaknesses, they enlisted the help of a very attractive woman called **Delilah**. She flashed her eyes and gave him her most dazzling smile. **Samson** yelled, 'This is a girl… for **SAMSON**!' and before long he'd asked her to marry him. They hadn't been married for long before **Delilah** began to ask **Samson**: '**Samson**, oh **Samson**! Tell me the secret of your superpowers.'

'My dearest darling **Delilah**,' replied **Samson**, 'I love you very much but I promised God I wouldn't tell anyone.'

But **Delilah** wouldn't take 'no' for an answer. She wheedled and wheedled and wheedled and wheedled (actually, **Delilah** was very good at wheedling!). Finally, **Samson** told her if she tied him up with bowstrings he'd lose his strength. (It was a lie, but then he really didn't want her to know.)

When **Samson** was asleep, **Delilah** tied him up with bowstrings good and tight. Then she yelled, '**Samson**! **The Philistines** are attacking!' Immediately, **Samson** woke, leapt to his feet and snapped all the bowstrings as though they were tissue! **Delilah** was really cross. She started to pester him again, and once more he gave in. He told her that if she tied him up with new ropes he'd lose his strength. (It was a lie again, but then he really didn't want her to know.)

When **Samson** was asleep, **Delilah** tied him

Reproduced with permission from *Collective Worship Unwrapped* published by BRF 2005 (978 1 84101 371 8) www.barnabasinschools.org.uk

up with ropes good and tight. Then she yelled, 'Samson! The Philistines are attacking!' Immediately, Samson woke, leapt to his feet and snapped all the ropes as though they were tissue! Delilah was really, really cross. She started to pester him again, and once more he gave in. He told her that if she tied his hair to a loom and nailed it to the wall, then he'd lose his strength. (It was another lie, but then he really didn't want her to know.)

When Samson was asleep, Delilah tied up his hair good and tight in a loom. Then she yelled, 'Samson! The Philistines are attacking!' Immediately, Samson woke, leapt to his feet and snapped all the strings as though they were tissue! Delilah was really, really, really cross. She started to pester him again, and once more he gave in. He told her that he'd made a promise to God and that if she cut off his hair he would lose his strength.

Delilah realized that he was finally telling her the truth, so she secretly sent for the Philistines. When Samson was asleep, she cut off all his hair! Then she yelled, 'Samson! The Philistines are attacking!' Immediately, Samson woke, leapt to his feet and yelled, 'This is a job… for SAMSON!' But it was no good. Without his hair he was powerless—superpowerless, in fact—and he felt as weak as a kitten!

The Philistines rushed in, overpowered Samson easily and—and this is the really awful bit—they blinded him and chained him up in their deepest darkest prison. There they made him a slave, grinding corn for their people. Poor Samson!

But while he was in the Philistine prison, Samson's hair started to grow again. He began to realize how wrong he had been to break his promise to God, and he prayed for a chance to make things right. One day, his chance came. The Philistines brought Samson into a huge temple arena so that they could all make fun of him in his blindness and slavery. There were thousands of Philistines and they all shouted at Samson and said that their god Dagon had helped them overcome God's superhero.

Meanwhile, Samson asked a small boy to guide his hands towards the huge pillars that held up the temple. Then Samson prayed one last time to God: 'Dear God, help me one last time. Restore my superpowers so that I can finally destroy your enemies.' Then Samson bowed with all his might on the huge pillars that held up the temple. His super-strength returned and the pillars crumbled. The temple collapsed and everyone was destroyed. God's enemies were defeated and Samson the superhero ended his life in victory.

Reproduced with permission from *Collective Worship Unwrapped* published by BRF 2005 (978 1 84101 371 8) www.barnabasinschools.org.uk

Mr Big's oven

STORYTELLING METHOD:

Audience participation

Bible link

Daniel 3:19–30

Nebuchadnezzar commanded some of his strongest soldiers to tie up the men and throw them into the flaming furnace... The fire was so hot that flames leaped out and killed the soldiers. Suddenly the king jumped up and shouted, 'Weren't only three men tied up and thrown into the fire?' 'Yes, Your Majesty,' the people answered. 'But I see four men walking around in the fire,' the king replied. 'None of them is tied up or harmed, and the fourth one looks like a god.' Nebuchadnezzar... said to the three young men, 'You servants of the Most High God, come out at once!' They came out, and the king's high officials, governors, and advisors all crowded around them. The men were not burnt, their hair wasn't scorched, and their clothes didn't even smell of smoke. King Nebuchadnezzar said: Praise their God for sending an angel to rescue his servants!

 Visual aids

❖ A tape or CD of some well-known theme music.
❖ Three large round homemade cardboard badges in different colours, labelled Shadrach, Meshach and Abednego.
❖ Three fairly confident-looking volunteers.
❖ A stern-looking adult.

Helpful hints
This is another assembly to employ full audience participation. It will also involve quite a bit of noise and activity so it might be a good idea to practise being quiet in response to a prearranged sign.

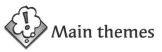 Main themes

Bullying and worship.

Further topics covered
Confidence, faith and trust, prayer.

 Prayer

Lord God Almighty, thank you that you are powerful and strong. Please give us courage when we feel scared. Amen

 Songs

I will raise my hands (KS)
Jesus, you are the king (KS)
My God is so big (KS)
Oi, oi, we are gonna praise the Lord (KS)

FOLLOW-UP

Have a discussion about worship. Point out that the word 'worship' suggests someone or something that we give 'worth' to. We give honour, respect, attention, reverence and so on to that person or thing. What people and things do some people worship nowadays? (Film, sport and pop stars, fashion, money, power, fame, popularity and so on.)

Discuss the pressure to conform to following a particular person, team, trend or fashion. How do we deal with that pressure? How and why should we worship God? Is that difficult to do nowadays? How hard is it to stand out from the crowd and be different?

Once… once upon… once upon a… once upon a time… once upon a time there was… once upon a time there was a king. He was a big king! He was an important king! He was a rich and famous and powerful king! But he was not a nice king. Oh no, not a nice king at all. His name was Nebuchadnezzar. Can you say that? No? I thought not. We'll just call him Mr Big.

Now, even though Mr Big was the biggest, most important, richest, most famous and powerful king in the world, he still was not happy. He thought he should be even bigger and more important than God, so he commanded that a huge statue, 27 metres high and 3 metres wide, looking just like him, should be set up and everyone in his kingdom should be made to worship it.

I tried to find someone really big and important to pretend to be the statue, so I asked *(insert appropriate name)* … but I could only find *(insert name of stern-looking adult)*.

The chosen adult stands at the front with their arms folded and a stern expression on their face. If they are willing, you could add a tall and imposing-looking hat on their head to complete the effect.)

Mr Big commanded that all his subjects assemble before the giant statue, and when they heard the sound of his special royal orchestra they should bow down and worship the statue. Anyone who did not do this would be immediately thrown into Mr Big's oven—a huge blazing furnace of fire, so hot it could have fried a snowman!

Now, among Mr Big's subjects were three men who were special friends of the living God. Their names were Shadrach, Meshach and Abednego. Do we have anyone here with those names? No? Oh well, I guess I'll just have to pick three people who I think are sitting quietly and listening carefully.

(Pick three confident-looking children and stand them at the front, to the side. Fasten the badges on them.)

Now Shadrach, Meshach and Abednego knew that they should not worship anyone or anything other than the Lord God Almighty—and that included Mr Big's statue. The only trouble was that if they refused to bow down, they all got thrown into the blazing hot oven! What should they do?

The music started up.

(Play the tape or CD. I used to use the theme from 'Dallas' but something more up-to-date would be better. 'Neighbours', 'Home and Away', 'Hollyoaks' or anything instantly recognizable to primary school-age children will do. Encourage the children to extend their arms out straight and begin bowing up and down from the waist until the music stops, making sure they are careful not to hit those around them. Don't 'fade' the music; shut it off suddenly.)

Everyone began bowing down to the gigantic statue of Mr Big—everyone, that is, except Shadrach, Meshach and Abednego.

(These three remain standing, unmoving.)

When Mr Big saw the three friends refusing to worship his statue, he became very angry and ordered his musicians to play again.

(Repeat the music, bowing and so on.)

Still the three friends refused to budge! Mr Big was so cross that his face grew red and he stamped on the floor until his feet hurt. Why wouldn't these three men worship his statue? Shadrach, Meshach and Abednego stepped forward and politely explained to the king that they wouldn't worship anyone or anything except the Lord God Almighty. 'If you don't worship my statue and my gods,' snarled Mr Big, 'I'll have all three of you thrown into my oven, and no god is powerful enough to save you from that!'

'Do what you have to, O king,' said the three friends. 'Our God will save us from your oven, but even if he doesn't we will not bow down or worship your statue or your gods!'

'This is your last chance,' yelled Mr Big, 'your very last chance. Face the music! Bow down when you hear it, or it's the oven for you!'

(Repeat the music, bowing and so on.)

Shadrach, Meshach and Abednego *still* refused to worship the statue! It was the last straw for Mr Big. He ordered the oven to be heated up seven times hotter. Now it was hot enough to fry three snowmen, in the Arctic, on a very cold day without their coats on. Mr Big's soldiers grabbed the three friends, tied them up and threw them fully clothed into the oven. It was so hot that the flames licked out and burned up the soldiers in a flash!

(You could add to the drama at this point by sending the three children out or placing them behind a screen or around a corner.)

Mr Big peered through the window in the side of his oven and, to his amazement, saw not three but four people walking around inside the flames. The fourth one looked just like… an angel! He ordered the oven door to be opened, and the three friends stepped out unharmed and untied.

(Bring the three children back into public view and encourage everyone to give them a round of applause as they go back to their places.)

Shadrach, Meshach and Abednego were not burnt, and their shoes and tunics and hats and coats were not burnt. They didn't even smell of smoke! God had saved them from the oven.

Mr Big was amazed. Now it was his turn to bow down and worship. But not to a statue. To God—the one, true, living God! He made Shadrach, Meshach and Abednego important officials in his palace because they had refused to dishonour God, and he commanded that everyone in his kingdom should worship the Lord God Almighty.

Sometimes it is hard to worship God when we are afraid or if someone tries to bully us, but God is always with us and he will help us to do the right thing. Shadrach, Meshach and Abednego were willing to obey and worship God even if he didn't save them from Mr Big's oven. Now, that's real courage!

Reproduced with permission from *Collective Worship Unwrapped* published by BRF 2005 (978 1 84101 371 8) www.barnabasinschools.org.uk

Storms

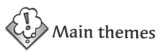

STORYTELLING METHOD

Audience participation

Bible link

Mark 4:35–41

That evening, Jesus said to his disciples, 'Let's cross to the east side.' So they… started across the lake with him in the boat… Suddenly a storm struck the lake. Waves started splashing into the boat, and it was about to sink. Jesus was in the back of the boat… asleep. His disciples woke him and said, 'Teacher, don't you care that we're about to drown?' Jesus got up and ordered the wind and the waves to be quiet. The wind stopped, and everything was calm. Jesus asked his disciples, 'Why were you afraid? Don't you have any faith?' Now they were more afraid than ever and said to each other, 'Who is this? Even the wind and the waves obey him!'

Visual aids

❖ Use overhead screen images of a storm to illustrate the story if you have them available.
❖ As an alternative, you could use different coloured modelling balloons to represent the wind, waves, thunder and lightning, and get children to hold them at the front.
❖ A vivid imagination and plenty of audience participation.

Helpful hints

This is a great assembly for plenty of noise and activity but it is vital to remember that the key point of the story is to emphasize Jesus' authority and the transition from noise and chaos to peace and safety. Prepare the children to be completely silent at a given signal and be sure to practise this several times before you begin the story.

Main themes

Faith and trust.

Further topics covered

Obedience, the power of nature, the authority of Jesus.

Prayer

Dear God, help us to trust you when we are afraid. Help us to know that you are in control. In the storms of life, be the peace that fills us always. Thank you, Lord. Amen

Songs

Be still and know (JP)
Life is like a big wide ocean (KS)
With Jesus in the boat we can smile at the storm (JP)

FOLLOW-UP

Talk about weather and the power of nature—hurricanes, whirlwinds, typhoons, tornadoes and tropical storms. Show a chart of the Beaufort Scale and get the children to imagine what it must be like to face each grade of wind. You will find information about the Beaufort Scale on the Met Office website, www.met-office.gov.uk.

Show some pictures of storms or storm damage, or possibly a sensitive extract from a movie such as *Twister*. Why do you think Jesus was able to control the storm on the lake? What kind of things might be like storms in our lives? How can God help us during these times?

Have you ever been in a really bad storm? I have!

(Here you could relate your own experience of being in a storm, whether on land or at sea. If you don't have, or cannot remember, a particularly dramatic storm experience, use an example from someone else's life. You could also make up a storm story, provided you make the children aware that it is a story.)

What do you find most scary about storms? The thunder? The lightning? The wind? In 1987 there was a terrific storm in Great Britain. The wind was so strong that they nearly had to change the name of Sevenoaks, a town in Kent, to Oneoak, because six of these landmark trees were blown over!

Did you know the Bible has a story all about a terrific storm that Jesus and his friends faced on a big lake near their home? Would you like to hear it? Well, OK, but I'm going to need your help to tell it properly. Let me see now… I could do with your help on the sound effects.

(You should get certain sections of the children to make wave noises [splish, splash, splosh], certain sections to make wind noises [woooo, woooo, woooo], certain sections to make lightning noises [kerrraccckkk!], certain sections to make thunder noises [kahboooom!] and the noises of the rain by slapping the tops of their thighs repeatedly faster and louder. Practise these noises, and don't forget to practise the 'being quiet' signal, ideally when Jesus says 'Be quiet!' coupled with you holding up your arms.)

Now the story begins …

Once upon a time Jesus and his friends decided to take a boat across the big lake near where they were staying. It had been a long day and Jesus had been working very hard, meeting lots of people and telling them all about the kingdom of God. He wasn't just tired, he was exhausted! No sooner had they set off than Jesus curled up in the back of the boat with his head on a cushion and fell asleep.

It was evening when the boat set off and everyone was a bit tired, otherwise one of them might have noticed that the weather was looking decidedly 'iffy'. Still, a good number of them were experienced sailors and nobody thought they had anything to worry about. They could not have been more wrong! By the time they reached the middle of the lake, the sky was looking rather dark and the waves were beginning to get bigger *(splish, splash, splosh!)* The wind started to pick up *(woooo, woooo, woooo!)* and tug at the sails and rigging, and a light rain began to fall *(slow and quiet slapping)*.

Then came the first rumble of thunder *(kahboooom!)* followed a few seconds later by a terrific flash of lightning *(kerrraccckkk!)*. The waves got bigger and the wind blew stronger and the thunder crashed louder and the lightning flashed brighter *(build the excitement with the sound effects getting louder)*. And do you know what? Through all this noise and chaos, Jesus stayed sound asleep!

The waves got even bigger and the wind blew even stronger and the thunder crashed even louder and the lightning flashed even brighter! By now, even the friends of Jesus who were sailors were frightened. They'd never seen a storm as bad as this. It was well scary! They all started to panic. Some were shouting. Some were yelling. Some were screaming. They were all terrified that the boat would turn over and they would all drown. And still the waves got bigger and the wind blew stronger and the thunder crashed louder and the lightning flashed brighter *(build the excitement with the sound effects getting even louder)*.

Then someone shook Jesus by the shoulder to wake him up. 'Lord!' they cried out. 'Don't you care if we all drown?' Jesus opened his eyes, stood up in the boat and in a loud voice called out:

PEACE! BE … QUIET! *(raise your arms)*

At once the wind stopped, the thunder and lightning stopped and the waves were calm. The rain just stopped in mid-air and disappeared!

(By now, you should be able to hear a pin drop, so remember to lower your voice and maintain the moment.)

'Why are you so afraid?' asked Jesus of his friends. 'Don't you trust me?' Jesus' friends were amazed, but do you know what? They never ever doubted Jesus again!

Reproduced with permission from *Collective Worship Unwrapped* published by BRF 2005 (978 1 84101 371 8) www.barnabasinschools.org.uk

All creatures great and small

Audience participation using visual aids

 ## Bible link

Psalm 139:13–14

You are the one who put me together inside my mother's body, and I praise you because of the wonderful way you created me. Everything you do is marvellous! Of this I have no doubt.

 ## Visual aids

- ❖ Some rubber animals such as beetles, spiders, bats, snakes, worms, earwigs, scorpions and so on.
- ❖ A hand-held mirror.
- ❖ A trick 'creepie-crawlie' (see below).
- ❖ A bag or box to hold these items.
- ❖ A blindfold.
- ❖ *The Weakest Link* theme music (optional).

FOLLOW-UP

This assembly provides a useful link to science and nature. You might like to link it to a mini-beast hunt (an outdoor trip to a wildlife park or conservation area, or just rooting around in the school grounds to see what you can come up with). It would also be a good opportunity to show some pictures of various creatures and discuss reactions to them. Where do they come from? Who made them? Who made us? How important are these creatures? How important are we?

Encourage plenty of drawing!

Helpful hints

Take special care when presenting the assembly to younger children who may focus too quickly on the 'fear' aspects. Prepare carefully and get teachers to recommend volunteers or to pick those who will handle the blindfold sequence without tears. I find that the 'game show' aspect works best with older children and adults, and the 'wonders and mysteries of nature' works better with younger children.

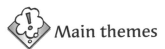 ## Main themes

Fear and self-esteem.

Further topics covered

Creation, self-worth, the world of nature, how we see each other.

 ## Prayer

Thank you, Lord God, for making us so special and for loving us so much. Please help anyone who is afraid or upset or who doesn't feel so special or loved. Help us to make them feel special and loved too. Amen

 ## Songs

Mr Cow (KS)
I'm special (KS)

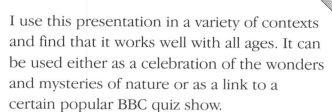

I use this presentation in a variety of contexts and find that it works well with all ages. It can be used either as a celebration of the wonders and mysteries of nature or as a link to a certain popular BBC quiz show.

Introduce the assembly by asking the children what they are afraid of and why. You could even interview an adult about their 'worst nightmare'. Then say that you are about to carry out an experiment in fear, and you would like six volunteers who are really brave. You can either call them out one by one or get all six to stand at the front.

Alternatively, you can ask for six contestants who would be willing to play *The Merest Blink*, the idea being that when you see the frightening thing you have been touching, you won't blink. The experiment/game then progresses in the following manner.

One by one, the volunteers are blindfolded and handed one of the rubber animals. To increase the excitement and anticipation, you need to build the suspense for the blindfolded volunteer by describing the frightening creature before you actually give it to them to hold. For example, 'Imagine you are on holiday in a villa in Spain. You wake up in the middle of the night, desperate for some lemonade. You creep into the kitchen in your bare feet to find the fridge. You don't want to disturb the others by putting the light on, so it's pretty dark in there. As you cross the kitchen floor, your bare foot comes down on something that scuttles and then goes 'crrrrunch'. 'It's a cockroach/beetle/earwig.

Each time a volunteer holds a creature and tries to guess what it may be, you may get a reaction or you may get none. Say 'Thank you' or 'You are the merest blink! Goodbye!'

and play the theme music. Make sure they get a round of applause.

The fifth volunteer usually gets the biggest fright, so you could use an adult for this one. Wind an elastic band tightly up inside a piece of card and tell your volunteer that this creature is a 'dried scorpion' and is so scary they don't have to wear a blindfold but just open up the card. As they do so, the tightly wound elastic spins round, making a startling sound and scaring them half to death.

As an alternative to dismissing everyone with 'You are the merest blink! Goodbye!' you might like to share some simple and amazing facts about some of the creatures and why they might not be as frightening as they first seem. *The Guinness Book of Records* can provide some interesting facts that will amaze the children.

The sixth volunteer is blindfolded and given a mirror. As you put on the blindfold, you tell them that this last creature is certainly the most amazing and wonderful in the whole world. You could disguise the feel of the mirror so that the volunteer won't realize what it is until you remove the blindfold and they look straight into the mirror.

You close by explaining to everyone that we are the crown of God's creation and that we are 'fearfully and wonderfully made' (Psalm 139). Emphasize the fact that we are special and that God loves us. Encourage some children to look into the mirror and say, 'I am special and God loves me.' You may be surprised by the reactions you get!

Reproduced with permission from *Collective Worship Unwrapped* published by BRF 2005 (978 1 84101 371 8) www.barnabasinschools.org.uk

Invisible seeds

STORYTELLING METHOD

Using the imagination

 Bible link

Galatians 5:22–24

God's Spirit makes us loving, happy, peaceful, patient, kind, good, faithful, gentle, and self-controlled. There is no law against behaving in any of these ways. And because we belong to Christ Jesus, we have killed our selfish feelings and desires.

Philippians 4:8

Finally, my friends, keep your minds on whatever is true, pure, right, holy, friendly, and proper. Don't ever stop thinking about what is truly worthwhile and worthy of praise.

 Visual aids

- ❖ An empty seed packet.
- ❖ Half a dozen or so large seed-shaped pieces of cardboard with words like 'Time', 'Hope', 'Encouragement', 'Love', 'Help', 'Forgiveness', 'Understanding', 'Joy', 'Kindness' and 'Care' written on them.
- ❖ A magician's 'flower' (one that you can stuff up your sleeve).
- ❖ A very vivid imagination.

Helpful hints

The beauty of this assembly is that it can be done without any visual aids at all. The key to the exercise is all in the imagination, as you persuade the children to 'see' what really isn't there. Encouraging them to do this helps them to appreciate the non-material world of concepts and ideas, thoughts and emotions. There is also scope for using an adult as one of your volunteers. It is good to remember that adults can get as much benefit from collective worship as children—and why not?

 Main themes

Harvest and witness.

Further topics covered

Helping others, the non-material world.

 Prayer

Dear God, please help us to plant good things in other people's lives. Help us to develop your good gifts in our own lives, so that we can grow up to be the kind of people you want us to be. Amen

 Songs

I am the apple of God's eye (KS)
I want to be a tree that's bearing fruit (KS)
Make me a channel of your peace (JP)

FOLLOW-UP

This assembly provides a good opportunity to talk about gardening. You might want to look at the school garden or set up a class project in growing some seeds from scratch. Cress is always very popular but sunflowers can be more spectacular over a period of time. You may want to show some gardening books or discuss types of gardening that the children are interested in.

It might be good to contrast the development of plants with the development of character. What do we need to produce strong and healthy fruit and vegetables? What do we need to produce strong and healthy attitudes? With older children you might like to discuss the 'fruit of the Spirit' as set out in Galatians 5:22–24.

This is a good assembly for harvest, so you might begin with a link to any fruit and vegetables on display and talk a little about how plants and flowers grow. Ask the children if they would like to grow some 'invisible seeds'. You just happen to have some with you! If you are using visual aids, you could now produce your empty seed packet. *(It is quite a good idea to make up a giant mock seed packet, perhaps with the title 'Gary Growrites AMAZING INVISIBLE SEEDS'. Insert your own name in place of the generic name. You could even write your crib notes on the back!)*

Peer inside the packet and inform the children that there are just a few seeds left, so they're in luck. Refer to the instructions on the back of the packet and list the invisible items that you will need to carry out the exercise. As you name each item, hunt round for it and then get a volunteer to come out and hold it. Since each item is invisible, you'll want to encourage the children to act up the pretence. 'Careful, you might drop it!' 'Now this one's a bit heavy so we'll need somebody with big muscles.' 'Are you sure you've got it OK?' and so on…

The invisible items are as follows:

1. An invisible pot.
2. An invisible bag full of invisible earth.
3. An invisible gardening fork or trowel.
4. An invisible watering can full of invisible water.
5. A big invisible bucket of invisible fertiliser.
6. The invisible seeds. (You can ask an adult to hold the invisible fertiliser and make a big scene about how bad it smells, making the volunteer stand over the other side of the hall and getting everyone to hold their noses!)

Once you've got all your volunteers out at the front, you can study your imaginary instructions and begin the planting exercise. The person with the bag of earth pours some of the earth into the invisible pot (being careful not to spill any!). The person with the fork or trowel makes an invisible hole in the earth and the person with the seeds carefully puts them into the hole and covers them up. Then the person with the watering can waters the earth, and the person with the fertiliser (phew!) spreads it over the top.

Keep the children's interest by constantly asking, 'Now, who's got the seeds?', 'Where's the person with the earth?', 'What do we do next?', 'Have I forgotten anything?' Getting this kind of interaction and participation enables the children to be more fully involved in understanding the assembly.

When all the instructions have been completed, there should be a brief moment of quiet anticipation. 'Now we wait six invisible months…' (Pause) '… which are fortunately shorter than real ones… and what do we get? Invisible flowers!' Since there is still nothing much to see except what is in the imagination, this should prove to be something of an anti-climax.

However… if you are using some visual aids, this is where you can bring them in. (You can still conclude the assembly without them.) You ask the children, including your volunteers, if they really believe that there are some invisible items in front of them. Most will probably say that they don't, and you initially begin to reinforce that belief by going through each item in turn—no invisible earth, no invisible water, no invisible pot and so on. Of course they don't really exist! However, when you finally mention the invisible seeds, you inform everyone that, actually, invisible seeds really do exist. You can either produce your cardboard seeds and get volunteers to hold them and children to name them aloud, or you can describe them and get the children to give examples.

You explain that, as we go about, we all sow invisible seeds into other people's lives. Some of these seeds can be good seeds and some can be bad seeds. What are some of the good seeds? Show the various cardboard 'seeds' or get the children to describe some good 'seeds'.

What do you imagine bad seeds might be like? The thing about sowing bad seeds is that all you produce is weeds! But the good seeds, the seeds of kindness, help, love, time, care, encouragement and so on… we sow them and they will produce flowers as beautiful as… these!

(Produce the magician's 'flower' from your sleeve or indicate a beautiful arrangement in the harvest display.)

Alternatively, explain that sowing good seeds produces beautiful characters and personalities. Indicate your volunteers and get them a round of applause as they sit down.

Jesus in the boot

STORYTELLING METHOD

Using mime

Bible link

2 Corinthians 5:17

Anyone who belongs to Christ is a new person. The past is forgotten, and everything is new.

Galatians 5:25

God's Spirit has given us life, and so we should follow the Spirit.

Visual aids

❖ Four chairs.
❖ An imaginative assistant.

Helpful hints
This is an assembly that requires careful preparation and rehearsal with your assistant.

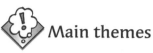
Main themes

Guidance and change.

Further topics covered
God's provision, witness.

Prayer

Dear God, thank you that Jesus can be with us always. Help us to trust him to help us and guide us always. Thank you, God. Amen

Songs

One more step (KS)
This little light of mine (KS)
With Jesus in the boat, you can smile at the storm (JP)

FOLLOW-UP

What does Jesus look like? What do we mean when we say that he is 'with us'? Is he really 'hiding in the boot of a car'? Why do some people not like talking about God?

Encourage drawings of Jesus and pictures of various forms of transport and ways God might guide us.

This is one of my oldest assemblies, but it is very effective if done right. You need just four chairs set up, two behind two, and an 'accomplice' to play the part of a non-speaking Jesus. You will need to rehearse the moves carefully together beforehand and, as with all mimes, you and your assistant need to get your movements just right. 'Jesus' needs to adopt an attitude that is neither patronizing nor overly comical—rather like a long-suffering parent who loves their child very much.

The story begins with 'Jesus' crouching down behind the two rearmost chairs. No reference is made to him (or her) at the beginning. You address the children something like this.

Good morning, everyone. I had a terrible time getting to school this morning! First of all, the car wouldn't start, and then I got lost and then… Look, I'll show you what I mean. Here's the car I came to school in.

(Indicate the four chairs. Your actions from this point must show that you really believe that these four chairs are a car. You walk round an imaginary bonnet, open an imaginary door and so on. Sit down and pretend to put the keys in the ignition and try to start the car. It works better without any sound effects or noises, the only sound being your voice doing a kind of commentary.)

Oh dear! It won't start! Whatever can be wrong with it? Now I'll never get to school in time for assembly today!

(Try again.)

No, still no good! What can I do? I know! I'll get Jesus out of the boot. He'll know what to do. He always helps me when I'm in trouble.

(Mime getting out, going round to the back of the car, opening the boot and helping Jesus out.)

Reproduced with permission from *Collective Worship Unwrapped* published by BRF 2005 (978 1 84101 371 8) www.barnabasinschools.org.uk

Oh, Jesus, there you are! I've got some real problems with the car. Can you help me, please?

('Jesus' gets out and opens up the bonnet, gesturing to you to try starting the car up again. Throughout the story, he acts calm and confident and determined. He doesn't speak at all but is clearly in control of the situation.)

Oh, that's great! Started first time. Thank you, Jesus. Now, back in the boot with you.

(Mime pushing Jesus back into the boot, which he accepts, albeit somewhat reluctantly. After this, you go through various stages—breaking down, getting lost and so on. Each time, you get Jesus out of the boot to help you. The next time, however, he insists on getting into the car on the back seat, although you do make him crouch down so he can't be seen. Then Jesus persuades you to allow him into the front passenger seat and finally to actually drive the car itself. Throughout this, Jesus remains patiently quiet and confident while you keep up a running commentary of what is going on.

When Jesus finally takes over control of the car, you sit next to him, jabbering excitedly about how wonderful it all is.)

Oh look, Jesus! There's some other people going the wrong way.

(Jesus nudges you and points straight ahead. It's clear that you need to keep your eyes on the road.)

Oh, sorry! Thank you, Jesus. We're going the right way now and we're sure to be on time. Whatever would I do without you?

Reproduced with permission from *Collective Worship Unwrapped* published by BRF 2005 (978 1 84101 371 8) www.barnabasinschools.org.uk

Arthur and the magic fish

Bible link

Luke 2:1–7

Joseph had to leave Nazareth in Galilee and go to Bethlehem in Judea. Long ago Bethlehem had been King David's home town, and Joseph went there because he was from David's family. Mary was engaged to Joseph and travelled with him to Bethlehem. She was soon going to have a baby, and while they were there, she gave birth to her firstborn son. She dressed him in baby clothes and laid him on a bed of hay, because there was no room for them in the inn.

Visual aids

❖ Some silly hats, scarves and so on can add to the fun if used in the right places, but the story can be told without props.

Helpful hints

This is an adaptation of a traditional folk tale, penned, I believe, by Leo Tolstoy. It is a very vigorous story with plenty of scope for audience participation and goes down well with all ages. Tell the story in a very animated way. Use lots of movement and build the story to a crescendo. If there are lots of children present, you might like to pre-plan a 'quiet moment' at the end, following a predetermined signal.

Here is a narrative that particularly uses the repetition device so favoured by storytellers. The repetition and the building of the excitement make the climax of the tale even more effective. You could use hats or costumes to illustrate Isabelle's different states or you could use children to act out the characters in the story. I find that a very deep-voiced fish, a rather timid and hesitant Arthur and a 'Sybil Fawlty' Isabelle work best.

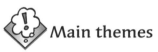

Main themes

Christmas and selfishness.

Further topics covered

Materialism, greed, riches, poverty, Third World issues.

Prayer

Dear God, help us not to be selfish and greedy. Thank you for sending Jesus to a poor and dirty stable in Bethlehem to remind us that friendship is more important than possessions and love is more valuable than riches. Amen

Songs

Away in a manger (JP)
Crackers and turkeys (KS)
See him lying on a bed of straw (KS)

FOLLOW-UP

What was the home of the greatest person who ever lived? What makes people great? What made Jesus great? Can anyone guess what was Isabelle's downfall? Which is more important—what we have or who we are?

Once upon a time, there was a man called Arthur. He was a fisherman. Sadly, he wasn't a very good fisherman, and he was so poor that he could only afford to live in a rickety old shack near the beach. Nevertheless, he was a simple and cheerful soul and his life would have been very happy were it not for one thing—his wife. She was called Isabelle and she never stopped moaning. All day long she criticized Arthur and complained about her lot. He was glad to go down to the beach and fish, if only to get away from her moaning.

One day, Arthur set off as usual for his regular fishing trip to the beach. The sun was shining brightly, the sky was blue without a cloud in sight, and the sea was as calm as a millpond. Arthur tossed in his line and waited for a bite. Almost immediately he felt a tug on the line and he reeled in a large and highly unusual rainbow-coloured fish.

Arthur took the huge fish in his arms and was just wondering how to get it home when the fish spoke! 'Hello, Arthur,' it said. Arthur stood open-mouthed as the fish explained to him that it was enchanted and could grant its captor any wish. The simple fisherman apologized to the fish and threw it back into the sea.

When he got home and told the story to his wife, she was not pleased. 'You stupid man!' she complained. 'Why didn't you wish for something? Go back at once and tell the fish I want to live somewhere nice. Tell it I want a cottage with a little garden and a nice lounge with a fitted carpet and a three-piece suite, and, and… a new dress!' So Arthur went back to the beach.

A few clouds were appearing in the sky now, and a light wind was causing a ripple across the water. Arthur stood on the shoreline and said this little rhyme. Say it with me, why don't you?

'Manye, manye, timpe tee, fishy, fishy in the sea, Isabelle, my wilful wife, does not like her way of life.'

Up popped the fish's head. 'Hello, Arthur,' it said. 'What is it now?'

'Oh, it's my wife,' said Arthur. 'She doesn't want to live in a rickety old shack any more. She wants a cottage with a little garden and a lounge and a…'

'Go back,' said the fish. 'She's there already.'

Back went Arthur. When he got home, what a sight met his eyes. The rickety old shack was gone and in its place was a lovely thatched cottage with a garden and rose bushes and a little wicket gate and garden path. Inside, Isabelle reclined on a new sofa, resplendent in a beautiful velvet dress. But do you think she was satisfied? No! As soon as Arthur got in, she started complaining. 'You stupid man!' she complained. 'This isn't good enough. I want more! Go back at once and tell the fish I want to live in a modern detached residence. With five… no, seven bedrooms, and new furniture and a butler and new clothes and… and money!' So Arthur went back to the beach.

The sky was grey and overcast now, and the wind was starting to whip up the waves. A light drizzly rain was falling but Arthur stood on the shoreline and said this little rhyme:

'Manye, manye, timpe tee, fishy, fishy in the sea, Isabelle, my wilful wife, does not like her way of life.'

Up popped the fish's head. 'Hello, Arthur,' it said. 'What is it now?'

'Oh, it's my wife,' said Arthur. 'She doesn't

Reproduced with permission from *Collective Worship Unwrapped* published by BRF 2005 (978 1 84101 371 8) www.barnabasinschools.org.uk

want to live in a little cottage any more. She wants a detached house with seven bedrooms and new furniture and a butler and…'

'Go back,' said the fish. 'She's there already.'

Back went Arthur. When he got home, what a sight met his eyes. The little cottage was gone and in its place was a very select modern detached residence in its own grounds. A butler answered the door, and inside was Isabelle dressed up to the nines, eating grapes from a silver dish and counting out fivers on to an ornate table. Do you think she was satisfied? No! As soon as Arthur got in, she started complaining. 'You stupid man!' she complained. 'This isn't good enough. I want more! Go back at once and tell the fish I want to live in a stately home with 50 bedrooms, and servants and a swimming pool and a Rolls-Royce and fur coats and jewels. Go back!' So Arthur went back to the beach.

The sky was dark grey and the rain was falling steadily. The wind was stronger and the waves were bigger. Arthur had to raise his voice as he said (say it with me):

'Manye, manye, timpe tee, fishy, fishy in the sea, Isabelle, my wilful wife, does not like her way of life.'

Up popped the fish's head. 'Hello, Arthur,' it said. 'What is it now?'

'Oh, it's my wife,' said Arthur. 'She doesn't want to live in a detached house any more. She wants a stately home with 50 bedrooms, and servants and a swim…'

'Go back,' said the fish. 'She's there already.'

Back went Arthur. When he got home, what a sight met his eyes. The modern detached residence was gone and in its place was a magnificent stately home. There was not one but three Rolls-Royces outside and an indoor

and an outdoor swimming pool. Servants were everywhere, and inside, Isabelle, dressed in silks, furs, gold and diamonds, was giving orders to everyone. But do you think she was satisfied? No! As soon as Arthur got in, she started complaining. 'You stupid man!' she complained. 'This isn't good enough. I want

more! Go back at once and tell the fish I want to be queen and live in a palace with gold and silver and jewels. Go back!' So Arthur went back to the beach.

The sky was black. The rain was falling in torrents. A mighty gale was blowing and the waves were 15 feet high! Arthur stood on the shoreline again and shouted:

'Manye, manye, timpe tee, fishy, fishy in the sea, Isabelle, my wilful wife, does not like her way of life.'

Up popped the fish's head. 'Hello Arthur,' it said. 'What is it now?'

'Oh, it's my wife,' said Arthur. 'She doesn't want to live in a stately home any more. She

Reproduced with permission from *Collective Worship Unwrapped* published by BRF 2005 (978 1 84101 371 8) www.barnabasinschools.org.uk

wants to be queen and live in a palace with gold and…'

'Go back,' said the fish. 'She's there already.'

Back went Arthur. When he got home, what a sight met his eyes. The stately home was gone and in its place was a huge palace. A fleet of cars was outside, alongside a purpose-built 18-hole golf course. Servants were everywhere, and inside, Isabelle sat on a large throne with a crown on her head and gold and jewels about her feet! Do you think she was satisfied? No! As soon as Arthur got in, she started complaining. 'You stupid man!' she complained. 'This isn't good enough. I want more! Go back at once and tell the fish I want to be emperor of the world and live in a magnificent golden temple with loads of money and jewels and furs and servants and… and everything! Go back!' So Arthur went back to the beach.

The sky was red. The rain was falling in floods! A hurricane was blowing and the waves were 50 feet high! Arthur stood on the shoreline again and shouted at the top of his voice:

'Manye, manye, timpe tee, fishy, fishy in the sea, Isabelle, my wilful wife, does not like her way of life.'

Up popped the fish's head. 'Hello, Arthur,' it said. 'What is it now?'

'Oh, it's my wife,' said Arthur. 'She doesn't want to be queen and live in a palace any more. She wants to be emperor of the world and live in a temple with money and…'

'Go back,' said the fish. 'She's there already.'

Back went Arthur. When he got home, what a sight met his eyes. The palace was gone and in its place was the most fantastic building he'd ever seen. It was a hundred feet high, made out of gold and studded with diamonds.

There were fleets of cars, swimming pools, golf courses and a 30-screen multiplex cinema! Even the servants had servants and everyone was bowing down to Isabelle. There she sat on a colossal throne 50 feet high, with a solid diamond crown on her head, surrounded by gold, silver, diamonds, rubies, emeralds, sapphires and precious stones! Do you think she was satisfied? No! As soon as Arthur got in, she started complaining. 'You stupid man!' she complained. 'This isn't good enough. I want more! Go back at once and tell the fish I want to live in the home of the greatest person who ever lived! Go back! Go back! Go back!' So Arthur went back to the beach.

The sky was black and red! The rain was falling in floods, torrents and waterfalls! There was a hurricane coming from one side and a whirlwind from the other and the waves were a hundred feet high! Arthur stood on the shoreline again and shouted at the very top of his voice:

'Manye, manye, timpe tee, fishy, fishy in the sea, Isabelle, my wilful wife, does not like her way of life.'

Up popped the fish's head. 'Hello, Arthur,' it said. 'What is it now?'

'Oh, it's my wife,' said Arthur. 'She doesn't want to be emperor of the world and live in a temple any more. She wants to live in the home of the greatest person who ever lived!'

'Go back,' said the fish. 'She's there already.'

Back went Arthur. When he got home, what a sight met his eyes. The huge temple was gone, the servants were gone, the cars and swimming pools and riches were gone. In their place was the rickety old shack and in the middle of it all, dressed in a dirty old sack, sat Isabelle. And serve her right!

Reproduced with permission from *Collective Worship Unwrapped* published by BRF 2005 (978 1 84101 371 8) www.barnabasinschools.org.uk

The man who wasn't there

This is simply a re-telling of the story of the road to Emmaus (Luke 24:13–35). I've got three different ways of telling it, which show three different methods of storytelling—character and costume, question and answer and visual aids and conjuring.

STORYTELLING METHOD

(Version 1)
Character and costume

Bible link

Luke 24:13–35

Two of Jesus' disciples were going to the village of Emmaus… Jesus came near and started walking along beside them. But they did not know who he was. Jesus asked them, 'What were you talking about as you walked along?' … Then the one named Cleopas asked Jesus, 'Are you the only person from Jerusalem who didn't know what was happening there these last few days?' … Jesus then explained everything written about himself in the Scriptures… When the two of them came near the village where they were going… they begged him, 'Stay with us! …' After Jesus sat down to eat, he took some bread. He blessed it and broke it. Then he gave it to them. At once they knew who he was, but he disappeared.

Visual aids

❖ A disguise for yourself, or a person (well-known to the children) who is disguised.

Helpful hints
This presents a good springboard into the area of 'stranger danger'. Be careful to make the distinction (especially with younger children) between strangers and those whom we do know but fail to recognize at first. Be sure to leave the children with a positive feeling rather than simply negative fears about strangers.

Main themes

Resurrection and truth.

Further topics covered
Easter, strangers, hospitality.

Prayer

Dear God, help us to recognize you working in our lives. Thank you that Jesus is alive today and that he can be our friend. Amen

Songs

From heaven you came (KS)
God's not dead (KS)
Lord of the dance (JP)

FOLLOW-UP

What kind of people are strangers? How should we behave towards them? (Keep away. Tell a teacher, parent, or someone you know well and trust.)

Who likes dressing up and pretending to be someone else? How does it feel? How can we recognize God at work even when we cannot see him?

Enter the assembly hall heavily disguised or, if you prefer, use someone the pupils know well (a teacher, perhaps) who is heavily disguised. They could be wearing anything from a wig and dark glasses to a mask. They could disguise their voice or put on an unfamiliar accent. Get the children to try to guess who the person is. Discuss how difficult it might be to recognize someone, particularly if it's dark or foggy or if they have done something to change their appearance.

Take the opportunity to refer to 'stranger danger'—that is, the need to be wary with strangers. Try to draw a distinction between strangers and those whom we know but fail to recognize at first. You can then simply tell the story of the two disciples on the road to Emmaus and how they 'recognized Jesus in the breaking of the bread'.

To add to the excitement and suspense, you might keep the 'unveiling' of your mystery guest until the point in the story when Jesus is revealed. If the mystery person has been you, you might have told the story in a different and mysterious voice. If the mystery person has been someone else, you might like to interview him or her about some aspect of the story. Conclude the narrative with the disciples' return to Jerusalem and their second meeting with Jesus in the upper room (Luke 24:36–49). Make the point that we often fail to recognize the truth even when it is right in front of our eyes.

The man who wasn't there

STORYTELLING METHOD

(Version 2)
Question and answer

Bible link

Luke 24:13–35

Two of Jesus' disciples were going to the village of Emmaus... Jesus came near and started walking along beside them. But they did not know who he was. Jesus asked them, 'What were you talking about as you walked along?' ... Then the one named Cleopas asked Jesus, 'Are you the only person from Jerusalem who didn't know what was happening there these last few days?' ... Jesus then explained everything written about himself in the Scriptures... When the two of them came near the village where they were going... they begged him, 'Stay with us! ...' After Jesus sat down to eat, he took some bread. He blessed it and broke it. Then he gave it to them. At once they knew who he was, but he disappeared.

Visual aids

❖ You may wish to use a blackboard/whiteboard or OHP to record the number of questions asked, although the story can be told with no props at all.

Helpful hints

Use something visual if you can. This assembly is mainly verbal and 'cerebral', so look for ways of keeping the interest of your hearers and don't let the brighter children dominate. Try using some of the children to keep score of the questions. Drop a few hints if things seem to be getting bogged down.

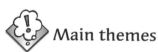

Main themes

Resurrection and truth.

Further topics covered

Easter, hard questions.

Prayer

Dear God, thank you that Jesus is the answer to so many hard questions. Thank you for making him come alive again after he was dead, to show us that even death is not the end. Thank you, God. Amen

Songs

As for version 1.

FOLLOW-UP

This is a good assembly to follow up with a question-and-answer session. The children could be primed to prepare questions that they wish to ask you about the Easter story. Alternatively, you could ask a local Christian (for example, the vicar/parish priest/minister/pastor) to come in and answer questions about their job and their life. I have personally found these kind of sessions very stimulating indeed. Expect questions like 'Are you allowed to get married?', 'Do you live in the church?', 'What do you like best about your job?', 'Do funerals make you sad?' and my personal favourite, 'What's your favourite colour?'

Sessions like this help to form a really good rapport between the school and the local church and can provide many ideas for future collaboration.

This version is based on the popular game 'Twenty Questions'. You briefly describe a scenario and your audience gets to ask a number of questions, to which you may only reply 'Yes', 'No' or 'Irrelevant'.

In this story, your scenario is: 'Three people went into a house but only two came out. What happened to the third person?' The scenario is, of course, the Emmaus story from Luke 24:13–35. You might like to 'warm up' the children with a couple of other exercises in lateral thinking. The most popular is: 'A man takes a car to a hotel, pays the owner of the hotel a large sum of money and then leaves. Explain why.' The answer is… he was playing the board game 'Monopoly'!

It may take your listeners several questions to discover the right answer but this will help to maintain their interest in the story.

When the pupils have discovered the identity of the third person, you could retell the circumstances that led to his disappearance and what happened afterwards. You might then take the opportunity to briefly explain the Easter message.

The man who wasn't there

 Bible link

Luke 24:13–35

Two of Jesus' disciples were going to the village of Emmaus… Jesus came near and started walking along beside them. But they did not know who he was. Jesus asked them, 'What were you talking about as you walked along?' … Then the one named Cleopas asked Jesus, 'Are you the only person from Jerusalem who didn't know what was happening there these last few days?' … Jesus then explained everything written about himself in the Scriptures… When the two of them came near the village where they were going… they begged him, 'Stay with us! …' After Jesus sat down to eat, he took some bread. He blessed it and broke it. Then he gave it to them. At once they knew who he was, but he disappeared.

Visual aids

❖ Some conjuring tricks, especially ones involving disappearance.
❖ Alternatively, the services of a friendly conjurer.

Helpful hints

'Magic' tricks are a sure-fire way of maintaining interest. Remember the value of audience participation and visual aids. There is great scope for both here.

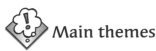 Main themes

Resurrection and truth.

Further topics covered
Easter, miracles and mysteries.

 Prayer

Dear God, thank you that Jesus is so powerful, he is even stronger than death. Thank you that his resurrection was not a trick but a real event that can bring hope for all the world. Amen

 Songs

As for version 1.

FOLLOW-UP

The whole area of 'magic' and mystery is a huge can of worms, but one that I believe needs to be opened up for primary school-age children. Key Stage Two and even Key Stage One are the *Harry Potter* and *Buffy the Vampire Slayer* generation and it does little good ignoring the influence of these and similar characters. Provided that you are sensitive to the age of your hearers, this can be a useful topic of conversation in a 'circle time' scenario as it gives you the opportunity to contrast the miraculous and supernatural elements of the Gospel narrative with the bogus 'magic' so often presented in society. Emphasize the truth of Bible stories (including the supernatural and miraculous elements).

If you know how to do it, this version is a good opportunity to use the old disappearing handkerchief trick. You'll need a flesh-coloured thumb stool and a small, brightly coloured silk handkerchief to carry this off. Most good 'magic' shops will sell you this trick, or one like it. Remember to practise carefully!

Alternatively, you could take the opportunity to invite a conjuror into school to amaze the pupils with a couple of simple tricks involving 'disappearance'. You can then tell the story of the man who wasn't there or the man who disappeared. As before, tell the story of the Emmaus road in your own words. Be sure to emphasize that Jesus wasn't a magician or wizard. His miracles were real because God's power was at work in him. By contrast, the 'magic tricks' that you or your friend have just done are exactly that—tricks that have a simple and logical explanation. (You might even like to show the children a simple trick that they can use to impress their friends.)

Make the point that Jesus rose from the grave to show his power over death. He 'disappeared' from the tomb to bring us hope and the possibility of new life.

Key Stage Two assemblies

Mob the maniac

STORYTELLING METHOD

Dramatic narration

Bible link

Mark 5:1–20

Jesus and his disciples crossed Lake Galilee and came to shore near the town of Gerasa. When he was getting out of the boat, a man with an evil spirit quickly ran to him from the graveyard where he had been living... He shouted, 'Jesus, Son of God in heaven, what do you want with me? ... Jesus asked, 'What is your name?' The man answered, 'My name is Lots, because I have "lots" of evil spirits.' ... Over on the hillside a large herd of pigs was feeding. So the evil spirits begged Jesus, 'Send us into those pigs! Let us go into them.' Jesus let them go, and they went out of the man and into the pigs. The whole herd... rushed down the steep bank into the lake and drowned... Then the people came out to see what had happened. When they came to Jesus, they saw the man who had once been full of demons. He was sitting there with his clothes on and in his right mind, and they were terrified... Jesus said, 'Go home to your family and tell them how much the Lord has done for you and how good he has been to you.'

FOLLOW-UP

Talk about fighting, wrestling, boxing and so on. Who usually wins? (The strongest, the fittest, the meanest, the biggest.) Jesus won his 'fight' without being any of these things. How did he do it?

What makes love such a powerful force? How did Jesus show his love for the world?

What happened to Mob immediately after he met Jesus? What happened after he went back to his home?

Visual aids

- ❖ A tape or CD of the drama.
- ❖ Pictures of the story on overhead projector to accompany the tape.

Alternatively, you could read the story from the drama, using voice characterization or an accomplice to vary the script.

Helpful hints
The nature of the story and the style of the dramatic narration makes this assembly really only suitable for older juniors. Use contemporary media stars of your choice as the commentators. You may wish to use visual stimuli as well as some audience participation to maintain interest. Pictures of boxing matches would be helpful if you have them. Check out the 'boxing match style' programmes that children watch nowadays, but use of them and reference to them will need to be handled very sensitively indeed.

Main themes

Overcoming violence and fear.

Further topics covered
Power and authority, good and evil, violence and aggression, bullying, love.

Prayer

Dear Lord, thank you that your power is stronger than any evil. Thank you that your love can overcome anything and change anyone. Amen

Songs

My God is so big (KS)
So we are marching along (KS)
When a knight won his spurs (KS)

Commentator 1: We welcome you on this hot, sultry morning to a packed house here at the Boneyard Coliseum for what promises to be a very interesting bout. And I see the MC is about to take his place and make the announcement.

MC: My lords, ladies, gentlemen… disciples and pig herders! *Mark Five Promotions* proudly presents the fight of the millennium—a one-round, no-holds-barred fight to the death. In the red corner, weighing in at a massive 390 pounds, from the Gerasenes, champion and current holder of the title 'Prince of this World', will you welcome Mob the Maniac! And his challenger, ladies and gentlemen, in the blue corner, from Cana in Galilee, representing himself… Jesus of Nazareth.

Commentator 1: Well, I can't see this bout going the distance. In all my years of professional commentating, I've never seen two men so mismatched. Mob, the local boy, has a string of fights behind him. He's never lost—probably due not so much to his size as to his incredible ferocity. He fights like a man possessed—a frightening sight. I must say the challenger looks hopelessly outclassed here, and yet he appears totally calm and oblivious to the danger. What do you think, Frank—has the newcomer from Galilee any chance here today?

Frank: Well no, Harry, not really. See… Mob's a really big boy and he fights hard. Know what I mean, Harry?

Commentator 1: Tell us about his unusual training programme, Frank.

Frank: OK, Harry; well, he lifts boulders and throws them around.

Commentator 1: Does he indeed?

Frank: Yes, I just don't know what's got into him, Harry. He breaks chains and hardens his body with stones. I've seen him take on five sparring partners at once. That's even more than Tyson. Know what I mean, Harry?

Commentator 1: So that accounts for the blood and those chains swinging from his wrists. But wait… the fight's about to start.

MC: Seconds away. Round one.

Commentator 1: And Mob the Maniac sees Jesus. He's running towards him. Jesus seems totally calm. He's not even taken his stance. He seems to be saying something. Mob has reached him. This is

Reproduced with permission from *Collective Worship Unwrapped* published by BRF 2005 (978 1 84101 371 8) www.barnabasinschools.org.uk

incredible! Mob the Maniac has fallen to his knees. He's shouting. This is amazing! He actually looks frightened. He appears to be begging for mercy. Jesus is talking to him… he's pointing… there seems to be some sort of disturbance on the hillside over to my left here. A large herd of pigs is… oh… back to the bout. Well, sensation here at the Boneyard Coliseum. It's all over. Mob is thanking Jesus. He's given in. The man from Nazareth has won. Incredible scenes here, David.

Commentator 2: Well, what an incredible result, er, Harry. Like nothing we've ever seen before. Absolutely astounding. This has to rank with the incredible marathon at, er, Marathon, I think, Harry.

Commentator 1: Well, I'm pushing through the crowds now to try and get a word with the former champion. Excuse me, sir.

Pig herder Oi! What about my pigs?

Commentator 1: Excuse me.

Pig herder Oi! I said, what about my pigs? I can't…

Commentator 1: Well, here is the former champion. And what a transformation, if I may say so. Hair brushed, face washed and clothes! Incredible! For the sake of those listening in black and white… a blue robe, brown sandals and a yellow sash. Well, former champion, what's your reaction?

Mob: I'm overwhelmed! This is wonderful! As long as I can remember, I've been crazy and full of anger and fear. But Jesus has set me free! I want to be his friend for ever.

Commentator 1: Well, there seems to be no sign of the man from Nazareth. I hear he's gone back across the lake.

Mob: Yes, I wanted to go with him, but he told me to stay and tell other people. I'm off to Decapolis right now to tell people my story.

Commentator 1: Do you think you'll get a hearing? After all, you've been held in fear for years.

Mob: I know it might be difficult at first, but once people see that I've changed, I'm sure they'll listen. You see, if Jesus can save me, he can save anyone. I just want to tell them all he's the best friend anyone could have, and that nothing is impossible for him.

Commentator 1: Well, thank you, Mob the Maniac.

Mob: No, Harry. I'm not Mob the Maniac any more. My real name is Eli. You can call me Eli the Evangelist!

Reproduced with permission from *Collective Worship Unwrapped* published by BRF 2005 (978 1 84101 371 8) www.barnabasinschools.org.uk

Peter the escape artist

STORYTELLING METHOD

Using visual aids

Bible link

Acts 12:1–19

King Herod put Peter in jail and ordered four squads of soldiers to guard him… While Peter was being kept in jail, the church never stopped praying to God for him… Peter… was asleep and bound by two chains… Suddenly an angel from the Lord appeared, and light flashed around in the cell. The angel poked Peter in the side and woke him up. Then he said, 'Quick! Get up!' The chains fell off his hands, and the angel said, '… follow me.' Peter left with the angel, but he thought everything was only a dream. They went past the two groups of soldiers, and when they came to the iron gate to the city, it opened by itself. They went out and were going along the street, when all at once the angel disappeared. Peter now realized what had happened, and he said, 'I am certain that the Lord sent his angel to rescue me from Herod.'

Visual aids

❖ Some chains, keys and padlocks.
❖ Pictures of Houdini or other famous magicians and escapologists.

Helpful hints
Either learn a simple escapology trick or get a local escapologist to demonstrate his or her art. You can end the assembly by emphasizing Peter's courage or the faith and steadfastness of the early Church. You could stress the power of prayer and explain how Christians believe that sometimes prayers are answered very quickly and dramatically. Or you could talk about habits and compulsions and discuss why Christians believe that Jesus can set us free from them.

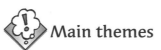

Main themes

Habits and prayer.

Further topics covered
Freedom from wrongdoing, angels.

Prayer

Lord God, thank you for sending your angel to help Peter escape from prison. When we feel trapped by our worries and fears, help us to know that you will help us. Amen

Songs

Be bold, be strong (KS)
God is good (KS)
Jesus, we celebrate your victory (KS)

FOLLOW-UP

This session might be a useful opportunity to talk about security and the need to keep property and belongings secure. You could have a display of keys, locks, padlocks and so on.

Ask the children how certain habits are like chains and prisons. Let them make the link between the two. Be prepared to talk about smoking and swearing and drugs. Ask them to suggest ways in which we could break certain habits. Ask if anyone has an example of a prayer that was answered.

Begin the assembly by asking the children to try to guess the secret identity of a famous person you are thinking of. To make it more interesting, you could have a silhouette on an overhead screen and slowly add some clues. The clues can be as follows:

1. His real name was Erich Weiss.
2. He was famous all over the world.
3. He was an entertainer who performed for presidents, kings and queens and the nobility.
4. He was a very popular magician.
5. His stage name is still widely known today.
6. He is the most famous escapologist ever (that means he was good at escaping from things).

The answer, of course, is Harry Houdini. You could describe some of Houdini's more amazing tricks and even refer to some of his modern-day imitators, such as David Blaine. This would be the point at which to demonstrate your own amazing escape routine or introduce your escapologist friend. After this, you are ready to tell the story of Peter's amazing escape from Herod's prison.

Once upon a time (about 2000 years ago, actually) the friends of Jesus were having a really bad time. An evil king called Herod Agrippa (the grandson of the King Herod who tried to kill Jesus) got hold of Peter and threw him into prison.

(Encourage the children to say 'Boo, hiss!' whenever Herod Agrippa's name is mentioned.)

Four squads of guards, each having four soldiers, were detailed to watch Peter and make sure he didn't escape. Peter was locked up in the deepest, darkest dungeon and chained to two guards—one on his right and one on his left. Outside the prison door were two more guards—one to watch the door and one to watch the other guard to make sure he didn't fall asleep! Outside was a huge thick wall surrounding the place, and a massive iron gate was the only way through. It was a prison that even Houdini would have a job escaping from! The evil king Herod Agrippa *(say the name quickly as though it were one word and don't forget the 'Boo, hiss!')* planned to put Peter on trial in front of all the people and see if he could have him killed.

Meanwhile, all Peter's friends in the church were praying hard for God to help him.

And… guess what? God did help! In the middle of the night, while Peter and his guards were fast asleep, an angel appeared and gave Peter a huge great nudge. *(Stage whisper)* 'Oi!' Peter woke with a start and, to his amazement, the chains on his wrists and ankles just fell off. The angel told Peter to put on his sandals and his coat and follow him. At first, Peter thought he must be dreaming. Although Peter was wide awake and the angel was talking to him, all the guards remained asleep and nobody noticed Peter's escape. The prison door opened and both the guards there were asleep as well. The angel led Peter out to the city and the massive iron gates opened all on their own. It was a trick that even Houdini would have been proud of, but God can do anything, and chains and guards and prison doors are no problem for him. Wouldn't Herod Agrippa *('Boo, hiss!')* be cross when he found out?

Suddenly the angel disappeared. Peter realized that this was no dream and that he was really free. He went straight to John Mark's house, where many of Jesus' friends were praying, and banged on the door. One of the friends, called Rhoda, heard the knocking and recognized Peter's voice. She was so excited, she forgot to let him in and ran upstairs to tell the others. They all thought she'd gone crazy. 'He's locked up in Herod Agrippa's *('Boo, hiss!')* dungeon,' they said, 'or else dead!' But she finally persuaded them to open the door, so they let Peter in and realized that God had answered their prayers. How thrilled and excited everyone was! Peter told them all about the angel and made them promise to pass on the good news.

Meanwhile, the soldiers were really puzzled when they woke up and found Peter gone. They couldn't understand how he'd managed to get through locked chains and barred doors. When Herod Agrippa *('Boo, hiss!')* found out, he was furious that he had nobody to kill. He was in such a bad temper that he had the soldiers killed instead and went off by himself to sulk.

Reproduced with permission from *Collective Worship Unwrapped* published by BRF 2005 (978 1 84101 371 8) www.barnabasinschools.org.uk

The Two Johns

This is a series of quick-fire sketches for older children. The two characters are my own invention, shamelessly based on the 'Two Rons' popularized by comedians Hale and Pace. I used to perform the sketches in DJs and shades with a friend who is 6'9". Since I am 5'3", we make an interesting pair! The dialogues work well because they are short, sharp and aggressive (in a humorous way) and convey a clear Christian message. Years later, I still bump into ex-pupils who remember the two Johns. With the enduring popularity of Del Boy and Rodney from *Only Fools and Horses*, these two Eastenders can make quite a topical contribution to collective worship.

The sketches are best played deadpan with a broad East End or south Essex accent. John 1 is the boss and John 2 is the stooge, thick as two short planks but with a heart of gold. They act in a very intimidating way but all the violence and aggression are by implication only. If your abilities don't run to this kind of acting, get a couple of likely characters to act the sketch and then follow it with your own two-minute epilogue. If the two Johns can sustain the act, all these sketches can be followed up with class work where pupils can interview the Johns, still in character.

 ## Visual aids

❖ For each assembly you will need two confident and imaginative actors dressed in DJs and shades.

Helpful hints

Try to get your two Johns to stay 'in character' from the moment they enter the school hall to the moment they leave. They are supposed to appear intimidating and scary (in a humorous way). Most of the time, when they are not performing, they can just stand at the side and look menacing.

The Two Johns:

An offer you can't refuse

Bible link

Psalm 24

The earth and everything on it belong to the Lord. The world and its people belong to him. The Lord placed it all on the oceans and rivers. Who may climb the Lord 's hill or stand in his holy temple? Only those who do right for the right reasons, and don't worship idols or tell lies under oath. The Lord God, who saves them, will bless and reward them, because they worship and serve the God of Jacob. Open the ancient gates, so that the glorious king may come in. Who is this glorious king? He is our Lord, a strong and mighty warrior. Open the ancient gates, so that the glorious king may come in. Who is this glorious king? He is our Lord, the All-Powerful!

1 Corinthians 3:16

All of you surely know that you are God's temple and that his Spirit lives in you.

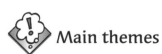

Main themes

Authority and environment.

Further topics covered
God's creation, the authority of the Bible, Third World issues, love, faith.

Prayer

Dear God, thank you for making the world and everything in it. We're sorry that we often make a mess of it and a mess of ourselves. Help us to trust you and put ourselves in your hands. Help us to read your book and follow you day by day. Amen

Songs

God loves all of his people (see page 12)
My God is so big (KS)
Shine Jesus, shine (KS)

FOLLOW-UP

This is a good opportunity for you (or preferably the two Johns) to have a classroom discussion on the value of God's love for us and our faith in him. Remember that the two Johns should remain 'in character'. You could also discuss views on creation: how was the world made, and how did we get here? You could then discuss how we handle the environment—a big topic with plenty of scope for project work and links to numerous other areas of the curriculum.

John 1: Allow me to introduce myself. My name is John and this is my…

John 2: … friend.

John 1: … associate… John. We represent the management. And he's not happy!

John 2: Right!

John 1: So we want you to listen… very carefully… otherwise we'll…

John 2: … nail your head to a coffee table!

John 1: … not be happy either! *(Glaring at John 2)* Now, the rule book is very clear.

John 2: VERY clear!

John 1: You have… read the rule book, I suppose? No? Oh, dear!

John 2: Oh dear, oh dear!

John 1: Oh dear, oh dear, oh dear!

John 2: Oh dear, oh dear…

John 1: *(Nudging John 2 very hard)* Now that makes us very sad. Right, John?

John 2: Right, John!

John 1: They haven't read the rule book. You know what that means, John?

John 2: They've transgressed the unwritten law!

John 1: *(Puzzled pause)* What unwritten law?

John 2: I dunno. They haven't written it yet.

John 1: Now, listen! The rule book says, 'The earth is the Lord's.' That means the management. Right, John?

John 2: Right, John!

John 1: But you've forgotten that. The book also says to look after the earth— but you don't! Right, John?

John 2: Right, John!

John 1: And it says your body is a temple, but you don't treat it right, do you?

John 2: Yes. *(Pause)* No!

John 1: Most of all—and this is what makes the management really unhappy— you've forgotten that the management *is* the management. Right, John?

John 2: Right, John!

John 1: So… we're here to make you an offer you can't refuse.

John 2: Right, John! *(Pause)* I'll get the chainsaw!

John 1: No! The management don't want you to treat them rough, John. You see, despite the fact you've broken the rule book, the management says he forgives you. Know what I mean? He really loves you! Yeah, I know it sounds cissy but listen… if you wanna be hard, I mean really hard, like me and John here… you've gotta love people what don't love you. Right, John?

John 2: Right, John!

John 1: And that's why we're here, representing the management, to make you an offer you can't refuse. Right, John?

John 2: Right, John!

John 1: And the offer we're making you is this. Put yourself in the hands of the management. Read his book. Hang out with him. 'Cos he wants to get to know you better. Right, John?

John 2: Right, John!

John 1: Trust the management. His name is…

1 and 2 together: God!

John 1: *(Stabbing out a finger)* Got it?

Reproduced with permission from *Collective Worship Unwrapped* published by BRF 2005 (978 1 84101 371 8) **www.barnabasinschools.org.uk**

The Two Johns:

Advent

 **Bible link**

Isaiah 40:30–31

Even young people get tired, then stumble
and fall. But those who trust the Lord will find
new strength. They will be strong like eagles
soaring upward on wings; they will walk and
run without getting tired.

 Visual aids

❖ To add to the pre-Christmas feel, John 2
could be carrying a wrapped present under
his arm.

 Main themes

Waiting and preparation.

Further topics covered
Advent.

 Prayer

*Thank you, Lord God, for Advent, a time
when I can get ready. Help us to be patient
and learn to wait, even when that is hard.
Thank you for the reminder that those who
wait get stronger in their trust of you. Amen*

 **Songs**

Be bold, be strong (KS)
O when the saints (KS)
So we are marching along (KS)
We are marching (KS)

FOLLOW-UP

This is another good opportunity for you (or preferably
the two Johns) to have a classroom discussion on the
value of God's love for us and our faith in him. Remember
that the two Johns should remain 'in character'.

What things do we have to wait for? What is the hardest
thing about waiting? How do you feel when you have to do
something that you are not ready for? What is it like to
'wait' on other people?

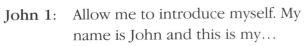

John 1: Allow me to introduce myself. My name is John and this is my…

John 2: … friend.

John 1: … associate… John. We represent the management.

John 2: Yeah! The management!

John 1: We are here to talk to you about…

John 2: Holly!

John 1: We are here to talk to you about…

John 2: Puddings!

John 1: We are here to talk to you about…

John 2: Turkey!

John 1: *(Loudly)* We are here to talk to you about Christmas!

John 2: Yeah! I can't wait till tomorrow to open my presents!

John 1: What?

John 2: Tomorrow, John. Christmas Day!

John 1: John… Christmas Day is 25 December. Tomorrow is *(give appropriate date)*!

John 2: But John, I can't wait till then, John. I'm too excited. Just think of all them presents!

John 1: You have to wait, John.

John 2: But I'm getting 'Tekken 4'. It's a pirate version—comes with a free parrot!

John 1: Get real, John! You can't celebrate Christmas on *(give appropriate date)*. It's too early. That's why we have Advent—to prepare!

John 2: Ad what?

John 1: Advent, John. You know what that is.

John 2: Yeah, John. It's a place where nuns live.

John 1: That's a convent, you wally! Advent is that special time of year that the management has designated as preparation time so we learn the importance of waiting. Right, John? … Right, John?

John 2: Sorry, John. I was waiting… for you to finish.

John 1: Don't try to be clever, John.

John 2: Sorry, John.

John 1: You see, what you lot have got to remember is that waiting and preparation is very important. You might want it all to happen now, like end of term, Christmas Day, summer holidays. But it don't work like that, do it, John?

John 2: No, John.

John 1: No, John. You have to wait—to get ready. That's what the Advent season is all about. Preparation is important because we have to get ready inside as well as out—for the things what are really important.

John 2: So I can't open my 'Tekken 4' tomorrow, John?

John 1: No, John. You have to wait. Like the management training manual says, 'Those what wait upon the Lord will renew their strength.' Right, John? *(Pause)*

John 2: *(Makes a muscle and smiles)*

Reproduced with permission from *Collective Worship Unwrapped* published by BRF 2005 (978 1 84101 371 8) www.barnabasinschools.org.uk

The Two Johns:

Christmas

Bible link

Matthew 2:1–15

When Jesus was born… Herod was king. During this time some wise men from the east came to Jerusalem and said, 'Where is the child born to be king of the Jews? We saw his star in the east and have come to worship him.' When King Herod heard about this, he was worried… Herod brought together the chief priests and the teachers of the Law of Moses and asked them, 'Where will the Messiah be born?' They told him, 'He will be born in Bethlehem…' Herod secretly called in the wise men and… told them, 'Go to Bethlehem and search carefully for the child. As soon as you find him, let me know. I want to go and worship him too.' The wise men listened to what the king said and then left. And the star… went on ahead of them until it stopped over the place where the child was…

When the men went into the house and saw the child with Mary, his mother, they knelt down and worshipped him. They took out their gifts of gold, frankincense, and myrrh and gave them to him. Later they… went back home by another road.

After the wise men had gone, an angel from the Lord appeared to Joseph in a dream and said, 'Get up! Hurry and take the child and his mother to Egypt! Stay there until I tell you to return, because Herod is looking for the child and wants to kill him.' That night, Joseph got up and took his wife and the child to Egypt, where they stayed until Herod died.

Main themes

Gifts and dedication.

Further topics covered
Christmas, Epiphany.

Prayer

Dear Lord, Christmas is your birthday. As we think about what would most make you happy today, help us to give the best of ourselves to become the people that you would have us be. Amen

Songs

I want to be a tree that's bearing fruit (KS)
The canticle of the gift (SOLW)
We three kings (JP)

FOLLOW-UP

The Two Johns could 'chair' a discussion on Christmas presents, starting with a competition such as: 'Who had the biggest present? Who had the smallest present? Who had the strangest present?' The Two Johns could give examples of their own presents (real or imaginary!).

What do you really want for Christmas? (You could vote for which gift everyone thinks is the best idea.) Is it better to receive presents or give them? Which is more fun?

Why do we give presents at Christmas? Is Christmas too commercial? Has it lost its true meaning?

What might it mean to 'give' yourself to God? What changes might it make in your life and daily routine?

If the class is small (or even if it isn't!) the two Johns might like to end this session by giving out some inexpensive Christmas gifts. These could be sweets or small books.

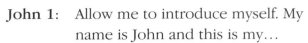

John 1: Allow me to introduce myself. My name is John and this is my…

John 2: … friend.

John 1: … associate… John. We represent the management.

John 2: Right! The management!

John 1: We're here today to talk to you about Christmas.

John 2: S'right. Christmas! The baby Jesus, the stable, the angels and the shepherds.

John 1: Right, John.

John 2: Mary and Joseph and the innkeeper.

John 1: Right, John.

John 2: The ox and the ass and the donkey and the flea.

John 1: Ri… ! What? There's no flea in the Christmas story!

John 2: Oh yes there is, John. *(Producing a really huge Bible and reading)* Mafew chapter two, verse firteen: 'Now when they had departed, behold, an angel of the Lord appeared to Joseph in a dream and said, "Rise, take the child and his mother and *flee*… to Egypt…"'

John 1: Oh yes, John. Very funny! All right, clever clogs. So what's a 'magi' then?

John 2: Ooo, I dunno that one, John!

John 1: It's the wise men, innit, John? You never mentioned them.

John 2: Oh, I remember. The free wise men! Yeah! *(Sings)* 'We free kings of Orient are, two on a camel and one in a car…'

John 1: *(Fingers in his ears)* All right, John, I fink we got the picture.

John 2: Hey, John. That could be us!

John 1: What?

John 2: The free wise men, John. If we had anuvver John, we could be the free wise men! *(Stands with a gormless, vacant smile)*

John 1: *(Looking at John)* No, John. I don't fink so. Anyway, how do you know there was free? There could have been more or less. The rule book says only that there was free special gifts.

John 2: Oh yes, that's right, John. Now don't tell me. Erm, gold… myrrh and… erm… Frankenstein.

John 1: Frankincense, John. Get it right!

John 2: Sorry, John!

John 1: Anyway, these guys came a long way to see Jesus. They'd read about him

Reproduced with permission from *Collective Worship Unwrapped* published by BRF 2005 (978 1 84101 371 8) www.barnabasinschools.org.uk

John 2: in the 'oly books and they knew he was going to be a great king, the saviour of the world.

John 2: Cor, that's clever.

John 1: That's why they was called 'wise' men... you plonker!

John 2: Oh.

John 1: And that's why they knew what gifts to give 'im. T'weren't no good giving him a PlayStation...

John 2: 'E'd 'ave nowhere to plug it in!

John 1: Right, John. They give 'im special gifts. Gold—because he was a king; myrrh—because he was going to be a sacrifice for the world...

John 2: And Frankenstein—because 'e liked 'orror stories?

John 1: No! Frankincense—because 'e was a priest. Stop messin' about, John!

John 2: Sorry, John.

John 1: The point is, John, Jesus wanted something more valuable than gold, more beautiful than frankincense and more special than myrrh. And he still wants that today.

John 2: What's that, John?

John 1: He wants you, John, you and me. We're more precious than all those gifts the wise men brought.

John 2: Really?

John 1: Straight up! *(Pointing to the children)* And that goes for you lot and all! Jesus wants you as a gift at Christmas.

John 2: Yeah, that's right. Don't bovver to wrap yourself up, come just as you are.

John 1: *(Looking at John 2, slightly surprised)*. Yeah, right, John. Absolutely right.

The Two Johns:

Lent

 Bible link

Luke 4:1–13

When Jesus returned from the River Jordan… the Spirit led him into the desert. For forty days Jesus was tested by the devil, and during that time he went without eating. When it was all over, he was hungry. The devil said to Jesus, 'If you are God's Son, tell this stone to turn into bread.' Jesus answered, 'The Scriptures say, "No one can live only on food."' Then the devil led Jesus up to a high place and quickly showed him all the nations on earth. The devil said, 'I will give all this power and glory to you… Just worship me, and you can have it all.' Jesus answered, 'The Scriptures say: "Worship the Lord your God and serve only him!"' Finally, the devil took Jesus to Jerusalem and had him stand on top of the temple. The devil said, 'If you are God's Son, jump off. The Scriptures say: "God will tell his angels to take care of you…"' Jesus answered, 'The Scriptures also say, "Don't try to test the Lord your God!"' After the devil had finished testing Jesus in every way possible, he left him for a while.

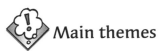 Main themes

Temptation and discipline.

Further topics covered

Lent, spiritual discipline, forgiveness, worship.

 Prayer

Dear God, help us to trust you more. Help us to resist temptation to do wrong and bad things. Please make us more like Jesus. Thank you. Amen

 Songs

Have you got an appetite? (KS)
When a knight won his spurs (KS)
My God is so big (KS)

FOLLOW-UP

Have a discussion about the difference between testing and temptation. (This could provoke a lively discussion, especially if there are school examinations in the offing! The simple answer is that the devil tempts us because he wants us to fail, whereas God tests us because he wants us to succeed.) Why do we have to take tests at school? What is the hardest test you have ever had to take? This is a good opportunity to talk about tests and exams in general, not just the ones at school.

Have you ever been tempted to do something wrong? How did you get on? This is a tricky area that needs to be handled sensitively. The Two Johns can treat the subject in a light but not insincere manner and be ready to move on if things get a bit 'heavy'. It is important to emphasize that everyone gets tempted, including mums and dads, teachers and even vicars! We only do wrong when we give in to temptation.

What can we do if we do give in to temptation? Is God cross with us? How can we make things right? This might be a good opportunity to gently raise the issue of forgiveness and how important it is to both give and receive it. You could finish the session with a quiet time of meditation and silent prayer.

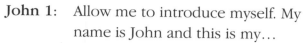

John 1: Allow me to introduce myself. My name is John and this is my…

John 2: … friend.

John 1: … associate… John. We represent the management.

John 2: S'right. So you better listen very carefully! Right, John?

John 1: Right, John.. We all need to listen. This is the season of Lent—a time of testing.

John 2: S'right. We will be coming round later to test all of you, to make sure you have been listening. And if you haven't, I'm going to put on my leather driving gloves and nail your head to a coffee table!

John 1: John! *John!* We don't do that no more.

John 2: What? No more coffee tables? Couldn't we just do it a little bit?

John 1: No!

John 2: How about breakfast bar?

John 1: No!

John 2: A small tea tray? I've got a nice one in the back of the car…

John 1: No, John! We don't nail people's heads to anything. The management don't like it, John. You know that.

John 2: Yes, John. Sorry, John. But we are going to test them, aren't we? You said it was a testing time.

John 1: Yes, John. That's because it's Lent.

John 2: What, like 'borrowed', you mean?

John 1: *(Deep sigh)* No, John. Lent is that special time of year, just before Easter, when we all try to become a bit more like what the management wants us to be.

John 2: What? Like becoming really cool and well hard, like what I am, John?

John 1: Not quite, John. It's all about discipline.

John 2: Now you're talking, John. *(Flexing his muscles and thumping his fist into his hand)* Giving 'em a good slap and sorting out round behind the bike sheds!

John 1: How many more times, John? If you want to be really hard, you've gotta love people! Discipline and testing is what Jesus did in the desert when he was tempted by the man downstairs!

John 2: Not the man downstairs! *(John 1 nods slowly)* What 'appened, John?

John 1: Well, the management knew Jesus was heading for a hard time and he had to be well strong. So he let the man downstairs test him. Jesus was really hungry and the devil tempted him to show off by turning some stones into bread.

John 2: I wouldn't be hungry in the desert, John. *(John 1 looks at him enquiringly)* I would eat the sand-which-is there! Get it?

John 1: Be serious, John! Jesus told the man downstairs what the rule book said about that, and how it was more important to follow God's word. Then the devil promised him the whole world if Jesus would only bow down and worship him.

John 2: Cor, I bet Jesus would like to have had the whole world, wouldn't he, John?

John 1: Maybe, John, but not that way! He knew you're only supposed to worship one person and that's the management. Finally, the devil tempted him to show off again by doing a Superman act off the top of the highest building he could find.

John 2: I bet he didn't try to copy Superman. You'd look really stupid with your underpants on the outside of your trousers!

John 1: *(Giving John 2 the look)* Jesus didn't fall for that one either. He knew he had to go God's way. So he told the man downstairs to shove off and stop bothering him.

John 2: And did he?

John 1: Certainly, John! Jesus is the guv'nor, right? You gotta do what he tells you.

John 2: I got tempted once, John.

John 1: Just once?

John 2: Well… lots of times actually. It's a bit embarrassing.

John 1: Don't be embarrassed, John. Everyone gets tempted, just like Jesus did, in lots of different ways. You can't help it.

John 2: But it's really hard not to give in, John. I can resist anything except temptation.

John 1: Well, do what Jesus did, John. Tell the devil to shove off. Every time you do, you'll get stronger!

John 2: Well, I'm pretty strong now, John.

John 1: You keep resisting the devil, John, and you'll be stronger than Superman, where it counts—inside!

The Two Johns:

Easter

 **Bible link**

Mark 16:1–8

After the Sabbath, Mary Magdalene, Salome, and Mary the mother of James brought some spices to put on Jesus' body. Very early on Sunday morning, just as the sun was coming up, they went to the tomb. On their way, they were asking one another, 'Who will roll the stone away from the entrance for us?' But when they looked, they saw that the stone had already been rolled away. And it was a huge stone! The women went into the tomb, and on the right side they saw a young man in a white robe sitting there. They were alarmed. The man said, 'Don't be alarmed! You are looking for Jesus from Nazareth, who was nailed to a cross. God has raised him to life, and he isn't here. You can see the place where they put his body. Now go and tell his disciples, and especially Peter, that he will go ahead of you to Galilee. You will see him there, just as he told you.' When the women ran from the tomb, they were confused and shaking all over. They were too afraid to tell anyone what had happened.

 Visual aids

❖ John 2 should be carrying a papier mâché model of the stone under his arm as though it weighs very little (which, of course, it does!).

 Main themes

Resurrection and help.

Further topics covered
Easter.

 Prayer

Dear Lord, thank you for coming alive again on Easter Day. Help us to realize that your love is bigger and stronger than anything, even death itself. Help us to trust you to help us, every day. Amen

Songs

Come on and celebrate (KS)
God's not dead! (KS)
I'm in right, outright, upright, downright happy in the Lord (KS)

FOLLOW-UP

This is a good opportunity for the two Johns to retell the Easter story (possibly the whole thing, if there's time) in their own words. You could also illustrate it further with selected clips from a commercial video or DVD such as *The Miracle Maker*.

Ask the children to share any problems they or their friends might have had. This might most appropriately be done through a circle time. (Be prepared to follow this up sensitively if particular issues arise.) Discuss how God might help us to overcome our problems, using the example of the resurrection story.

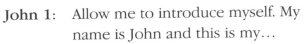

John 1: Allow me to introduce myself. My name is John and this is my…

John 2: … friend.

John 1: … associate… John. We represent the management.

John 2: S'right. So you better listen very carefully! Right, John?

John 1: Right, John!

John 2: Otherwise, I'll come out there and drop this dirty great rock on your heads! Got it?

John 1: No, John.

John 2: What?

John 1: No, John. They haven't got it. You've got it!

John 2: *(Suddenly looking at the 'rock' under his arm)* Oh, yeah! Right. I have.

John 1: And it's not real either, John, is it?

John 2: It's a dirty great, big, ugly, hard, heavy rock.

John 1: John, it's not real. It's made of paper.

John 2: But…

John 1 suddenly pushes the 'rock' from underneath and it pops out from under John 2's arm and falls on the floor. John 2 just looks at it.

John 1: See? It's… not… real. Got it?

John 2: No, I haven't. It's on the floor, John.

John 1: Right, John! And that's where you'll end up if you don't pay attention.

John 2: Sorry, John. So why did you give me that dirty great rock… sorry, dirty great lump of paper, then?

John 1: It's a visual aid, John!

John 2: What's a visual aid, John?

John 1: Somefink to help us remember.

John 2: Remember what, John? I fink I've forgotten.

John 1: *(Deep sigh)* What time of year is it, John? Think… chocolate eggs, fluffy bunnies.

John 2: Erm… Easter?

John 1: Right, John! And what happened at Easter?

John 2: Erm… Jesus, erm, died and they put him in a tomb.

John 1: A tomb with a…?

John 2: A tomb with a… with a… with a dirty great big piece of paper over it!

John 1 gives him the look.

John 2: Sorry, with a dirty great big rock over the front of it. Much bigger than this one *(pointing at the paper 'rock' on the floor)*.

Reproduced with permission from *Collective Worship Unwrapped* published by BRF 2005 (978 1 84101 371 8) www.barnabasinschools.org.uk

John 1: And much heavier, too! This was a real rock. The soldiers rolled it there and posted a guard over it, too.

John 2: Why, John? Jesus was dead. Dead people can't escape from tombs. They're… well, they're dead!

John 1: Right, John. But these soldiers thought Jesus' friends might come and steal the body and pretend he'd come alive again, like they'd said he would. And the soldiers would do anyfink to stop that!

John 2: Did they come, John? Did they steal the body?

John 1: Course not, John! They couldn't get past the guards and they certainly couldn't shift that rock. No—the management intervened personally. He sent one of his angels…

John 2: Right! The 'eavy mob! They're real strong, them geezers!

John 1: Right, John. So this angel puts the guard to sleep—nothin' aggressive, you understand—then, he just rolls that rock away, easy as you like. Jesus comes back to life, comes out of the tomb… Bob's your uncle!

John 2: Frank!

John 1: What?

John 2: My uncle, John. His name's Frank!

John 1: *(Giving John 2 another look)* The point is, John, if God can deal with a situation like that—massive rock… bolshi guards… dead body—don't you fink he could deal with anyfink you've got to worry about, no matter how big or heavy it is?

John 2: Right, John. *(Picking up the 'rock' and throwing it up in the air a couple of times)* So God can handle anything in our lives and help us deal with it, no matter how big or heavy it is, 'cos he is really kind and strong and even more powerful than death?

John 1: You got it!

John 2: *(Hugging the 'rock' and nodding vigorously)* Yes, John. I have!

Reproduced with permission from *Collective Worship Unwrapped* published by BRF 2005 (978 1 84101 371 8) www.barnabasinschools.org.uk

The Two Johns:

The occult

 ### Bible link

Philippians 4:8

Finally, my friends, keep your minds on whatever is true, pure, right, holy, friendly, and proper. Don't ever stop thinking about what is truly worthwhile and worthy of praise.

Helpful hints

This assembly and the later one on Hallowe'en are tricky areas to cover. It is important to try to get the balance right between the seriousness of the topic and the light-hearted way in which the two Johns deal with it. If done properly, this can convey a really important message at a time when the occult and the supernatural have a powerful effect on young people. You would do well to do a little background reading on the subject. (One or two books are listed at the back of this resource.)

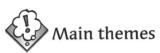 ### Main themes

The supernatural and truth.

Further topics covered
The occult, purity.

 ### Prayer

Dear God, help us to know that you are truth and light and goodness. Protect us from all that is evil and let us walk always in your ways. Thank you, God. Amen

 ### Songs

Jesus, we celebrate your victory (KS)
The Spirit lives to set us free (KS)
We are marching (KS)

FOLLOW-UP

This is a good opportunity to emphasize the truth of Bible stories (including the supernatural and miraculous elements) as opposed to the 'virtual reality' of popular fiction.

Talk about some of the fantasy-type programmes that are so popular on cable and satellite (*Buffy, Angel, Charmed, Dark Angel, Stargate, Star Trek* and so on… the list is endless) and also some of the recent movies that deal with the same kind of subjects. Find out what it is about these dramas that is so appealing to young people. Ask what positive messages the stories convey. Then ask what negative messages they may convey. Is there any reality behind the fantasy and how can we avoid becoming fascinated by evil and wrong?

Be sure to end on a positive note—possibly a short trivia quiz on a favourite fantasy show or a poll to find the children's favourite character.

John 1: Good morning. My name's John and this is my… my… my… er… friend, John, and we represent the… the…

All through this, John 2 has been staring ahead with a fixed expression on his face.

John 1: Oi! John. What's going on?

John 2: Do do do do… do do do do… do do do… *(music from 'The Twilight Zone')*

John 1: Oh no! What is it now?

John 2: *(Still looking blank)* I've been traumatated, John!

John 1: Do what?!

John 2: I've entered the unseen psychic zone that reaches from the inner mind to… THE OUTER LIMITS!

John 1: What are you going on about, John?

John 2: *(Seeming to suddenly snap out of his hypnotic state)* The outer limits, John… the twilight zone! *(Nods wisely)* Is the parrot normal.

John 1: Hmmm. I don't like the sound of this, John.

John 2: Oooo… my old mother swears by it. She always does her horoscope in the stars and she still reads her tea leaves, John.

John 1: And what *does* she read in her tea leaves, John?

John 2: PG Tips. Best before October 2006.

John 1: *(No reply)*

John 2: That was a joke, John.

John 1: It's no joke, John. This is serious stuff.

John 2: Too right, John. When I was at school we done the weejie board once. Cor… it weren't half spooky. You know what it said?

John 1: No John… and I don't want to know, neither!

John 2: Oh… well, I think it's great. My old mother's mother was a clair… clair wotsit… you know—cross your palm and look in the crystal ball.

John 1: Was she good at it?

John 2: Oh, you know… medium… *(Laughs)* Get it, John? Medium! *(Laughs)*

John 1: *(Deadly serious)* It's no laughing matter, John.

John 2: *(Quietening down)* Oh. Why not?

John 1: The management don't like it, John. The rule book says we shouldn't dabble in it.

John 2: What… the outer limits?

John 1: NO! Don't mess with horoscopes, ouija boards, séances and all that. Not at school, not at home, not—nowhere!

John 2: Why not? It's just a bit of harmless fun.

John 1: Sometimes, John. And sometimes… its dangerous! I know some people it's really messed up. It ain't just superstition—it can be real bad. Like these videos—Friday the 13th… all that Elm Street rubbish.

John 2: Oh, yeah… that film gave me bad dreams for weeks…

John 1: Well, don't watch it, then! And steer clear of the occult… Right, John?

John 2: Right, John!

John 1: The management says *(opening a Bible)* 'Finally, my friends, keep your minds on whatever is true, pure, right, holy, friendly, and proper. Don't ever stop thinking about what is truly worthwhile and worthy of praise.'

Reproduced with permission from *Collective Worship Unwrapped* published by BRF 2005 (978 1 84101 371 8) www.barnabasinschools.org.uk

The Two Johns:

Pentecost

Bible link

Acts 2:1–12

On the day of Pentecost all the Lord's followers were together in one place. Suddenly there was a noise from heaven like the sound of a mighty wind! It filled the house where they were meeting. Then they saw what looked like fiery tongues moving in all directions, and a tongue came and settled on each person there. The Holy Spirit took control of everyone, and they began speaking whatever languages the Spirit let them speak. Many religious Jews from every country in the world were living in Jerusalem. And when they heard this noise, a crowd gathered. But they were surprised, because they were hearing everything in their own languages… Everyone was excited and confused. Some of them even kept asking each other, 'What does all this mean?'

Visual aids

- ❖ A large brightly coloured balloon (preferably helium-filled and on a string).
- ❖ Some party decorations such as party hats, streamers, party poppers and so on.
- ❖ A large sign saying 'Happy Birthday'.

Helpful hints
Well stocked party shops will be able to provide most of the party equipment. The balloon does need to be as large as possible and brightly coloured. It should also be plain.

Main themes

Celebration and being special.

Further topics covered
Pentecost, festivals.

Prayer

Dear God, thank you for the gift of your Holy Spirit to live in us and be with us always. Help us to follow you and celebrate the life you give us. Amen

Songs

Come on and celebrate (KS)
God loves all of his children (see page 12)
Spirit of the living God (JP)

FOLLOW-UP

This assembly provides a good opportunity to have some fun with balloons. If you are following it up with the two Johns staying 'in character', they need to either have a competent balloon modeller with them or be able to do some themselves. After teaching the children to blow up balloons and make a few animals and so on, you can talk about where the breath of life comes from and how God breathed into his creation to give it life (Genesis 2:7). Explain that in some ancient languages 'breath' and 'spirit' are the same word. Say that our word 'inspire' comes from the Latin word for breath and means to breathe air into the lungs, but also to enthuse.

Explain how it is the invisible air (or gas) that gives 'life' to the balloon and determines its size and shape. How does the 'breath of God' in us determine our 'shape'?

John 1: Allow me to introduce myself. My name is John and this is my…

John 2: … friend.

John 1: … associate… John. We represent the management.

John 2: Yeah, that's right. The management. Yeah!

John 2 is wearing a party hat. He is draped in streamers and is holding on to the string of a large brightly coloured balloon.

John 1: John?

John 2: Yeah?

John 1: What's going on?

John 2: 'Appy birfday to me, 'appy birfday to me, 'appy birfday dear John, 'appy birfday to me!

John 1: What are you on about, John?

John 2: It's me birfday, John! I'm havin' a big party wiv all me mates. I got the streamers, look, and the fancy hat. I've even got these.

John 2 pulls out a couple of party poppers and lets them off. John 1 just looks bored.

John 2: And look, John, what else I got.

John 2 pulls out a large brightly coloured banner with the words 'Happy Birthday' or even 'Happy Birthday John' on it. He tries to unravel it and spread it out, enlisting the assistance of John 1, who gives in rather half-heartedly.

John 2: Yeah! It's me birfday! All day! 'Appy birfday to me, 'appy birfday to me…

John 1: John. *John!*

John 2: 'Appy birfday to me, 'appy birfday to me…

John 1: JOHN! 'Ow old are you?

John 2: Er… twenty-one… and a bit.

John 1: Yeah, right! Now there's a funny thing.

John 2: Ha, ha, ha, ha, ha, ha… *(Suddenly serious)* What's funny?

John 1: Well, it just happens to be our birfday, too!

John 2: No.

John 1: Yeah.

John 2: No!

John 1: Yeah!

John 2: N…

John 1: I said it is, John, and it is!

John 2: Really? Well, how old are you, then?

John 1: Two fousand.

John 2: Do what?

John 1: I said two fousand years. Two fousand years old.

Reproduced with permission from *Collective Worship Unwrapped* published by BRF 2005 (978 1 84101 371 8) www.barnabasinschools.org.uk

John 2: Blimey, John, you don't look it! You bin working out or somefink?

John 1: Not me personally, you plonker! I mean us, the organization, the Church! We bin around for about two fousand years.

John 2: Cor! That's great. We should have a party.

John 1: We do, John. Every Sunday.

John 2: Brilliant. So do we like get presents and everyfink for this birfday?

John 1: Course we do, John, you wally. The management gives us the 'Oly Spirit to fill us and be wiv us for ever! Two fousand years ago, the 'Oly Spirit came to celebrate the birf of the Church and now he comes to live inside everyone who follows the management.

John 2: Wot, so he's inside me right now? *(Looking inside his shirt)* I can't see him!

John 1: Course not, John, you nurf! He's invisibule, you can't see him!

John 2: How do I know he's there, then?

John 1: Look at your balloon, John. You know it's got somefink inside it but you can't see it, can you?

John 2: No, John.

John 1: But you know it's there 'cos it makes a difference outside!

John 2: Yeah!

John 1: And it's exactly the same wiv us.

John 2: Oh… yeah!

John 1: It don't matter what size, shape or colour you are…

1 and 2 together: *(To the audience)* … it's what's inside that counts!

Reproduced with permission from *Collective Worship Unwrapped* published by BRF 2005 (978 1 84101 371 8) **www.barnabasinschools.org.uk**

The Two Johns:

Harvest

 ## Bible link

Genesis 8:20–22

Noah built an altar where he could offer sacrifices to the Lord. Then he offered on the altar one of each kind of animal and bird that could be used for a sacrifice. The smell of the burning offering pleased God, and he said: Never again will I punish the earth for the sinful things its people do. All of them have evil thoughts from the time they are young, but I will never destroy everything that breathes, as I did this time. As long as the earth remains, there will be planting and harvest, cold and heat; winter and summer, day and night.

 ## Visual aids

❖ The largest pair of Y-fronts or boxer shorts you can find.
❖ A spoof 'shopping list'.

Helpful hints
A backdrop of harvest produce—fruit and vegetables, bottles, packets and tins—will help set the scene.

 ## Main themes

Thanks and provision.

Further topics covered
Harvest, God's provision.

 ## Prayer

Dear God, thank you for the harvest and all the good things you give us. Help us to remember to say 'thank you' to you and to those around us. Amen

 ## Songs

Give thanks with a grateful heart (KS)
Jehoveh Jireh, God will provide (KS)
Thank you, Lord, for this fine day (JP)

FOLLOW-UP

The Two Johns could spend some time talking about 'attitude' and the different kinds of attitude that we adopt—respectful, showing off, know-it-all and so on. They could then discuss how we might develop a 'gratitude attitude'. How would this mean we behaved?

What things specifically could we be grateful for? What should we say to people to show our gratitude? What kind of things could we do to show how much we appreciate other people? Perhaps the class could end by putting together a card collage or a home-made gift to give to a member of staff or someone else to say 'thank you'.

John 1: Good morning. My name's John and this is my…

John 2: … friend.

John 1: … associate… John! We represent the management—right, John?

John 2: Right, John!

John 1: Right! Today we've come to talk to you about 'arvest!

John 2: *(Producing a large pair of Y-fronts)* And ar pants!

John 1: Do what??

John 2: Ar vest and pants, John. What would we do without 'em?

John 1: John… John! We are talking about *h*arvest!

John 2: Oh… oh! Er… what's *h*arvest then, John?

John 1: Harvest thanksgiving, John, is when we say a big 'thank you' to the management for all the things he's given us.

John 2: What, like these real hard jackets and these dead cool shades?

John 1: No, John. I mean things like sun and rain, flowers and fruit and vegetables.

John 2: Oh… like my old muvver's cauliflowers.

John 1: Right, John.

John 2: And her radishes and taters.

John 1: Right, John.

John 2: Spring onions and greens. Free pound of tomaters, two tins of beans.

John 1: John… John?

John 2: Honeydew melon, a packet of Bird's Eye boil-in-the-bag cod in butter sauce, two tins of shoe polish, a…

John 1: John!

John 2: Sorry, John. Me muvver's given me a list for Safeways. I just remembered…

John 1: Well… remember this, John. All them things have been given us by the management. Right, John?

John 2: Right, John!

John 1: *(Pointing to the children)* And you lot would do well to remember it an' all!

John 2: Yeah!

John 1: Harvest reminds us that the management made a world full of good things for us to enjoy

John 2: *(Reading list)* Like cauliflowers, radishes, taters, tomaters, Bird's Eye boil-in-the bag…

John 1: Put the list away, John.

John 2: Right, John! *(Stuffs list into his pocket)*

John 1: Listen! The rule book says, 'As long as the earth endures, seedtime and harvest, cold and heat, summer and winter, day and night will never cease.' Good news, eh?

John 2: Right, John.

John 1: And all we need to do is remember to say 'thank you'. It don't hurt to say 'thank you' now and again.

John 2: Thank you… *(Looks around, cringing slightly, as if expecting to be hit)* You're right, John, it don't hurt! Thank you… Thank you… Thank you… Thank you.

1 and 2 together: THANK YOU!

The Two Johns:

Hallowe'en

 Bible link

1 Peter 5:6–11

Be humble in the presence of God's mighty power, and he will honour you when the time comes. God cares for you, so turn all your worries over to him. Be on your guard and stay awake. Your enemy, the devil, is like a roaring lion, prowling around to find someone to attack. But you must resist the devil and stay strong in your faith. You know that all over the world the Lord's followers are suffering just as you are. But God shows undeserved kindness to everyone. That's why he appointed Christ Jesus to choose you to share in his eternal glory.

 Visual aid

❖ A Hallowe'en mask.

Helpful hints

This assembly and the earlier one on the occult are tricky areas to cover. It is important to try to get the balance right between the seriousness of the topic and the light-hearted way in which the two Johns deal with it. If done properly, this can convey a really important message at a time when the occult and the supernatural have a powerful effect on young people. You would do well to do a little background reading on the subject. (One or two books are listed in the resources section on page 128.)

 Main themes

The supernatural and truth.

Further topics covered
Hallowe'en.

 Prayer

Dear God, help us to follow the way of truth and goodness and to stay away from all that is false and bad. Please protect us from anything that may harm us or cause us to turn from you. Thank you, God. Amen

 Songs

I am a new creation (KS)
The Spirit lives to set us free (KS)
This little light of mine (KS)

FOLLOW-UP

The Two Johns could ask if anyone has done trick or treat. Did you dress up? Was it fun? How did people respond to trick or treat? What are some 'treats'? What are some 'tricks'? How sensible is it to knock on people's doors at night? What about 'stranger danger'? In what ways could Hallowe'en be 'dangerous' or 'evil'? Why do we like to be scared?

The Two Johns could end by telling the story of Jesus' temptation in their own style (Matthew 4:1–11; Mark 1:12–13; or Luke 4:1–13) and offering some alternative suggestions for celebrating 31 October.

John 1: Good morning. My name's John and this is my…

John 2: … associate.

John 1: *(Looking at John)* … friend… John.

John 2: Cor! Thanks, mate. *(Puts his arm round John)*

John 1: Just watch it, right.

John 2: Sorry John. Er, John?

John 1: Yeah. What?

John 2: *(Putting on Hallowe'en mask)* Trick or treat? *(Takes off the mask)*

John 1: Urrggh! Put the mask back on, John.

John 2: We had them round last night, John.

John 1: What… masks?

John 2: No, John. The trick or treaters. Big spotty kid in a witches' mask. Didn't half give my poor old muvver a turn.

John 1: Yeah?

John 2: Yeah. She thought it was the Avon lady.

John 1: Not a good idea, trick or treat, John. Not good at all.

John 2: No, John? Why not?

John 1: The guv'nor don't like it, John. He don't like it at all.

John 2: But Hallowe'en's great, John. Ugly pumpkins, witches on broomsticks—everybody does it.

John 1: But we ain't everybody, John. We're the guv'nor's, we belong to the management.

John 2: Oh. But… but it's all just a bit of harmless fun, ain't it, John?

John 1: Maybe… and maybe not. You heard of the occult, John?

John 2: Yeah. I went to hear them at Wembley Arena. Got all their CDs.

John 1: No John. It's not a band. It's evil.

John 2: Oh, they're not that bad. The lead singer's a bit naff but…

John 1: John! Hallowe'en is a festival for the man downstairs!

John 2: *(Gasps)* Not the man downstairs!

John 1: Too right, John. And you know Jesus don't take no nonsense from him. Trick or treat used to be a way of paying off evil spirits in the old days, so what's the point in going round frightening people today? Is there really any point in scaring someone half to death?

John 2: *(Suddenly)* Boo!

John 1: *(Jumps, then gives John 2 a really long glare)* Listen, you lot. Hallowe'en can be just a bit of harmless fun, but messing with the occult is dangerous. Right, John?

John 2: Right, John! Definitely right. The man downstairs is no joke, believe me.

John 1: The management… he says, 'Fill your minds with good things, not horrible. Think about and say and do what's nice, what's helpful, what's pleasing to him.' Messing with evil don't do no one any favours… John?

John 2: Yeah?

John 1: Trick or treat?

John 2: Neither, John. I think I'll just stick with Jesus.

John 1: Good man.

Reproduced with permission from *Collective Worship Unwrapped* published by BRF 2005 (978 1 84101 371 8) www.barnabasinschools.org.uk

The Two Johns:

The prodigal

 ## Bible link

Luke 15:11–24

Once a man had two sons. The younger son said to his father, 'Give me my share of the property.' So the father divided his property between his two sons. Not long after that, the younger son... left for a foreign country, where he wasted all his money in wild living. He had spent everything, when a bad famine spread through that whole land. Soon he had nothing to eat. He went to work for a man... to take care of his pigs. He would have been glad to eat what the pigs were eating, but no one gave him a thing. Finally, he came to his senses and said, '... I will go to my father and say to him, "Father... I am no longer good enough to be called your son. Treat me like one of your workers."'

The younger son got up and started back to his father. But when he was still a long way off, his father saw him and felt sorry for him. He ran to his son and hugged and kissed him. The son said, 'Father... I am no longer good enough to be called your son.' But his father said to the servants, 'Hurry and bring the best clothes and put them on him. Give him a ring for his finger and sandals for his feet. Get the best calf and prepare it, so we can eat and celebrate. This son of mine was dead, but has now come back to life. He was lost and has now been found.' And they began to celebrate.

Helpful hints

This is probably the most serious and emotional of the two Johns' sketches and comes across very much like a personal testimony. Be prepared to field some questions on some big issues—life, death, sex, family, relationships. The language is slightly graphic in places. You may choose to tone parts of it down to suit your audience.

 ## Main themes

Forgiveness and relationships.

Further topics covered
Personal faith, wrongdoing, life and death, family, love.

 ## Prayer

Dear God, help us to know that no matter how badly we behave, you will always be willing to forgive us and help us start again. Show us your love right here and right now. Thank you, Lord. Amen

Songs

I'm accepted, I'm forgiven (KS)
I'm special (KS)
I will enter his gates (KS)

FOLLOW-UP

Do you ever feel so bad that you think you can't be forgiven? What happens when you let someone down? What if it's your mum or dad or your best friend? How can you make things right again? How can we make a new start?

This might be a good opportunity for a circle time on the subject of being sorry and saying sorry. Be aware of personal problems that may arise and make provision for sensitive follow-up.

John 1: Good morning. My name's John and this is my associate, John.

John 2: I think that they know who we are by now, John. I mean, after all, it isn't like we're complete strangers, is it? We've been coming here for some time, haven't we? Representing the management and all that. They know my name is John and yours is John an'…

As John 2 rabbits on, John 1 tries to interrupt. Finally he pulls John 2's head down and gives him the look.

John 2: Sorry, John.

John 1: Right, we are here to…

John 2: … represent the management, right?

John 1: Right, John, and don't interrupt me again. Right?

John 2: Sorry John. John…

John 1: Yeah, what?

John 2: Don't you ever do anything wrong, John? You always bin very clever and good, like you are now?

John 1: No John, I used to be a right little dipstick. Never did nothin' right. Down the clubs every night giving it plenty of this and that. Going to work with the spray can. I hate graffiti now.

John 2: Me too. I don't like any Italian food.

John 1: My poor old mother—she never knew where I was from one minute to the next.

John 2: Does she like cauliflower?

John 1: Some nights I never came home at all. I was always in trouble with the old bill.

John 2: I never got on too well with old Bill myself. Smelly old geezer.

John 1: Anyway… one night I got stoned out of me head. Nicked some cash out me mother's bag. The old dear

Reproduced with permission from *Collective Worship Unwrapped* published by BRF 2005 (978 1 84101 371 8) www.barnabasinschools.org.uk

had just come up on the bingo. She must have had nigh on 800 quid. I took the lot.

John 2: You never!

John 1: I did! Well, I hot-wired the old man's Merc and headed off for the big lights. Cor, you should have seen me at Clanceys Casino. I was on a bender. The women… the booze…!

John 2: Cor! I bet it was great.

John 1: No, John, it was sick. My mother died that night. I didn't even know. Seems the shock of me running off once again was too much for her heart.

John 2: *(Just looks at John)*

John 1: So, while I was sleeping it off, my old dad was saying goodbye to his missus. I saw the funeral announcement in the paper a week later. I was washing pots for Eric the Greek. All me money was gone. Me so-called friends, too. Eric let me have a few scraps off the plates. Cor, I hated houmous! Anyway, I begged a fiver off Eric and caught a bus to the cemetery. Got there as the funeral was finishing. I remember it clear as day—me dad standing by the grave, twisting his cap round in his hands. Then he looked at me. I knew at that moment what a berk I'd been—how I'd let me family down time after time. Me dad turned away… I knew things would never be the same again.

John 2: I bet he never spoke to you again, John—after all you'd done. The money, the car… your poor old mother.

John 1: I don't like thinking about it, John. But you're wrong. My dad turned away, but only to say something to the vicar. Then he said, 'Come here, boy.' I started to say, 'Dad, I'm so sorry… but he put his arms round me and said, 'Come home, son—we lost you but now you're back. That's all that matters.' From then on we started to get to know each other a whole lot better.

John 2: *(Sniffing and wiping his eyes)* Cor, what a story. You know what? That's just like the management, ain't it? God feels that same way about us. He'll always take us back if we're willing to change.

John 1: You know, John—you ain't as daft as you look.

John 2: Right, John.

Reproduced with permission from *Collective Worship Unwrapped* published by BRF 2005 (978 1 84101 371 8) www.barnabasinschools.org.uk

Appendix 1

THE TOOLSHED GANG OVERHEAD VISUALS

Billy the Big Hammer

Clara the Chisel

Sammy the Screwdriver

Paula the Pliers

Oily Fred

Pontifex the Power Saw

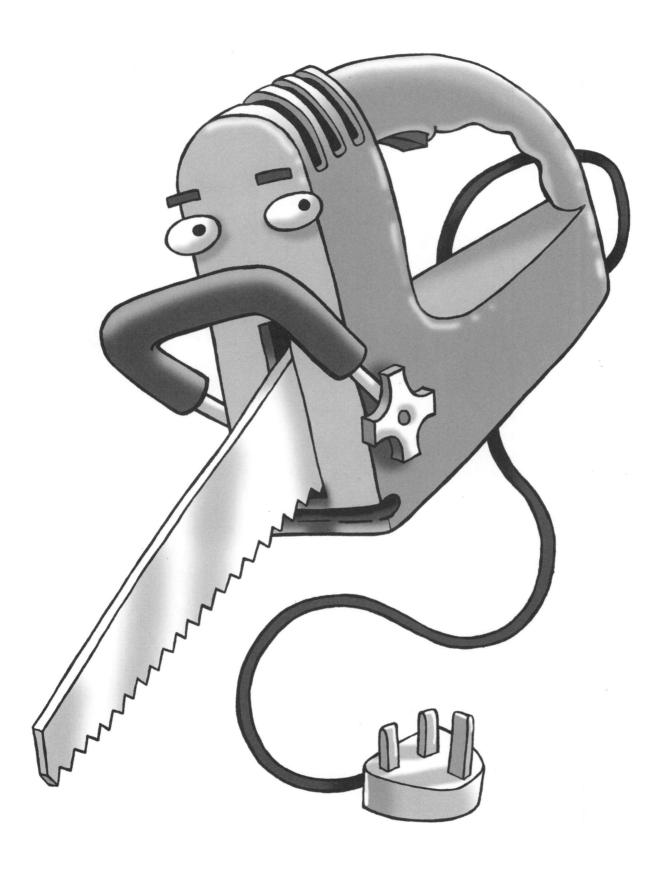

Timmy the Tile Cutter

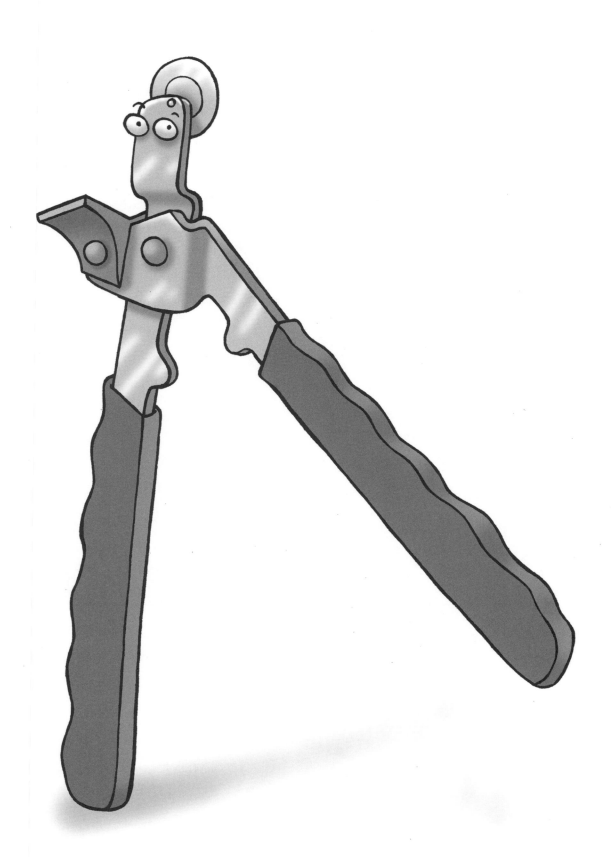

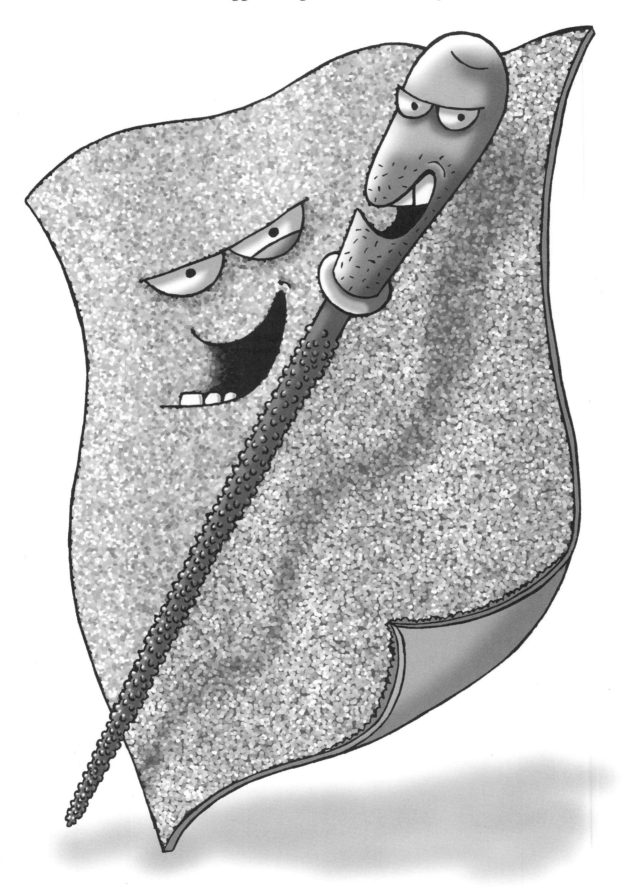

The Master Builder

Honky the Donkey

Reproduced with permission from *Collective Worship Unwrapped* published by BRF 2005 (978 1 84101 371 8) www.barnabasinschools.org.uk

Big Bad Brian the Lion

Full index of themes

Index of Bible links

Resources

SONG BOOKS FOR COLLECTIVE WORSHIP

Alleluya! 77 songs for thinking people with piano accompaniment and chords for guitar, David Gadsby and John Hoggarth (A&C Black, ISBN 9780713619973)

The Big Book of Spring Harvest Kids Praise (ICC, ISBN 9781873613078)

Brown Bread and Butter—70 songs, rhymes and games for children, Alison McMorland (Ward Lock Educational, ISBN 9780706241969)

Children's Sunny Day Song Book, Burt Brewis (International Music Publication, ISBN 978 863594670)

Come and Praise Books 1 & 2, Geoffrey Marshall-Taylor with arrangements by Douglas Coombes (BBC Educational Books published at the request of the Educational Broadcasting Council, ISBN 9780563342496)

Come and Sing, more Christian songs for under 8s, Ann Broad, (Scripture Union, ISBN 978 0854219483)

Eileen Diamond Super Song Book for children aged 3–7 (Universal Edition London Ltd, ISBN 9780900938719)

Every Colour under the Sun, songs on thoughtful things for primary school assemblies (Ward Lock Educational Ltd, ISBN 97807062 42660)

Oxford School of Music Books Infant Book, J.P.P. Dobbs and Winifred Fur (Oxford University Press, ISBN 9780193211001)

Also, many good 'singalong' songs are to be found on www.scoutxing.com including 'God's love is like a circle' to the tune 'Puff the Magic Dragon'.

USEFUL BOOKS

Badger's Parting Gifts, Susan Varley (Collins Picture Lions, ISBN 9780006643173)

God Is Always With Me, Helen Caswell (Lutterworth Press, ISBN 9780718827960)

Love You Forever, Robert Munsch (Firefly Books Ltd, ISBN 9780920668375)

Storytelling—A Practical Guide, Lance Pearson (Scripture Union, ISBN 9781859990940)

Halloween, Trick or Truth (Crossways Books USA, ISBN 9785551227519)

Halloween: What's a Christian To Do?, Steve Russo (Harvest House, ISBN 9781565078512)

The Facts on Halloween, John Anderberg and John Weldon (Harvest House, ISBN 978073691207)

To obtain information about tracts and posters on Hallowe'en, visit the CPO/Monarch Publishing website at www.cpo-online.org.uk.

MISCELLANEOUS

Up Up & Away (modelling balloon suppliers)
17 Newlands End
Basildon
Essex SS15 6DU
Tel: 01268 411712
Fax: 01268 541171
email: enquiries@upupandaway.co.uk

Unit 1
Wellington Park Estate
Waterloo Road
Staples Corner
London NW2 7UA
Tel: 0208 8452 9700
Fax: 0208452 6900
Website: www.upupandaway.co.uk